Documents and Debates
Social Conditions and
Welfare Legislation, 1800–1930

Documents and Debates
General Editor: John Wroughton M.A., F.R.Hist.S.

Social Conditions and Welfare Legislation, 1800–1930

George Ayres

MACMILLAN
EDUCATION

© George Ayres 1988

First published 1988

Published by
MACMILLAN EDUCATION LTD
Houndmills, Basingstoke, Hampshire RG21 2XS
and London
Companies and representatives
throughout the world

Typeset by Wessex Typesetters
(Division of The Eastern Press Ltd)
Frome, Somerset

Printed in Hong Kong

British Library Cataloguing in Publication Data
Social conditions and welfare legislation,
1800–1930.—(Documents and debates).
1. Great Britain—Social conditions—
19th century   2. Great Britain—Social
conditions—20th century
I. Ayres, George   II. Series
303.4'84   HN385
ISBN 0–333–40882–9

Contents

General Editor's Preface

This book forms part of a series entitled *Documents and Debates*, which is aimed primarily at sixth formers. The earlier volumes in the series each covered approximately one century of history, using material both from original documents and from modern historians. The more recent volumes, however, are designed in response to the changing trends in history examinations at 18 plus, most of which now demand the study of documentary sources and the testing of historical skills. Each volume therefore concentrates on a particular topic within a narrower span of time. It consists of eight sections, each dealing with a major theme in depth, illustrated by extracts drawn from primary sources. The series intends partly to provide experience for those pupils who are required to answer questions on documentary material at A-level, and partly to provide pupils of all abilities with a digestible and interesting collection of source material, which will extend the normal textbook approach.

This book is designed essentially for the pupil's own personal use. The author's introduction will put the period as a whole into perspective, highlighting the central issues, main controversies, available source material and recent developments. Although it is clearly not our intention to replace the traditional textbook, each section will carry its own brief introduction, which will set the documents into context. A wide variety of source material has been used in order to give the pupils the maximum amount of experience – letters, speeches, newspapers, memoirs, diaries, official papers, Acts of Parliament, Minute Books, accounts, local documents, family papers, etc. The questions vary in difficulty, but aim throughout to compel the pupil to think in depth by the use of unfamiliar material. Historical knowledge and understanding will be tested, as well as basic comprehension. Pupils will also be encouraged by the questions to assess the reliability of evidence, to recognise bias and emotional prejudice, to reconcile conflicting accounts and to extract the essential from the irrelevant. Some questions, *marked with an asterisk*, require knowledge outside the immediate extract and are intended for further research or discussion, based on the pupil's general knowledge of the period. Finally, we hope that students using this material will learn something of the nature of historical inquiry and the role of the historian.

John Wroughton

Acknowledgements

The author and publishers wish to thank the following who have kindly given permission for the use of copyright material:

Frank Cass & Co. Ltd for extracts from *Moral and Physical Condition of the Working Classes in Cotton Manufacture* by J. P. Kay, reprinted 1969; Eyre and Spottiswoode for extracts from *English Historical Documents Vol. XII (1)* edited by Young and Hancock and *(2)* edited by Hancock; and *Public Acts of the Realm*; Lawrence and Wishart Ltd for an extract from 'Song of Polly Parker' from *Folk Song in England* by A. L. Lloyd, 1969; Thames and Hudson Ltd for an extract from *Notes on England* by Hippolyte Taine, translated by E. Hyams, 1957.

Every effort has been made to trace all the copyright holders but if any have been inadvertently overlooked the publishers will be pleased to make the necessary arrangement at the first opportunity.

The author wishes to extend special thanks, for the help and support received to the following: Dr P. T. Woodland, Mr G. T. Goodall, the Governors of Exeter School, Dr R. W. Truman and Mr D. J. Dyson.

Introduction

By the time of the Great Exhibition in 1851 Britain was populous, powerful and rich; yet the generation of great national wealth, based on the profound changes in the British economy wrought over the previous half century, brought wealth for some and misery for others. A society formerly dominated by the traditional institutions of village, parish and manor threatened to be overwhelmed by great towns and powered industry. Of Britain's rapidly growing population there were many who faced problems of redundant skills; mechanisation and steam power brought the subdivision of labour and the need for semi-skilled or unskilled, cheap, docile labour to supervise the forces of production. The factory system made other difficulties: at work, long hours of toil, dangerous machinery, poorly designed and maintained buildings as well as noise and air pollution and inadequate sanitation; at home, in houses cheaply and quickly constructed, without planning or regulation, families were overcrowded and surrounded by 'nuisances' which weakened health and shortened life. These changes came upon a society ill-prepared intellectually or institutionally to meet them.

Contemporaries saw the central problem of the time as poverty, but relief of the poor was based upon the laws of settlement which essentially presupposed a stable and static society. A system devised for late-Tudor England was hardly adequate for the modern purpose. In the late eighteenth and early nineteenth centuries it was emphasised that the individual was master of his own fate and the local community could secure its own needs. Self-help and *laissez faire* were the rallying cries of the moment. Always, however, there were those who could not help themselves: the aged, sick, orphans, the indigent and impotent poor simply would not go away. It was expected that others would offer help and assistance. Philanthropy came from many directions; from the Quakers Elizabeth Fry and John Howard, from those who wished to return to a purely agrarian society like William Cobbett, from paternalists who thought it their Christian duty to give direction and benefaction, like the Earl of Shaftesbury. The activities of such as these were encouraged by the religious revivalism of the time. Evangelicals of the established church like Henry Thornton, Hannah More and William Wilberforce gave generously to philanthropic works; they, like their non–conformist counterparts, created a new moral outlook. Pragmatist advice came from Sir James Kay-Shuttleworth who warned that if the higher classes did not come to the aid of the lower, then the latter's 'misery, vice and prejudice will prove volcanic elements by whose explosive violence the structure of society may be destroyed'.

Commerce, industry and, increasingly, parliament, were deeply influenced by the ideas of political economy. Adam Smith, in *The Wealth of Nations*, wanted to 'liberate mankind from the restrictive and archaic panoply of arbitrary government'. His ideas of a free market were taken over by entrepreneurs and merchant communities; they saw justification for their own emphases on untrammelled initiative and enterprise together with a free market in labour. Smith's belief in *laissez faire* certainly did have limits: the state, he thought, ought to provide those services which others, individual or corporate, did not. Developing the same view as Adam Smith, that civil law is restrictive of human enterprise and creativity, Bentham introduced the concept of utility. While those laws which prevented the enjoyment of the greatest happiness of the greatest number had to be removed, state action, he thought, was needed. Unlike Ricardo he could not support the abolition of the Poor Law. He believed that necessary laws, based upon sound general principle, applied by rational administrative structures and universally enforced, alone could be effective: the watchwords were efficiency, integrity and centralised uniformity.

Bentham's rationalist approach to government was adopted by several of the dominant administrators of the day; Edwin Chadwick was outstanding among them. For the Benthamites accurate knowledge was essential; reports and statistics flowed from committees and commissions. Efficiency, economy and direction were provided by central boards, inspectors and other experts. They moulded the moral and social outrage generated by the humanitarians into solutions of their own shape. Government in the modern style was created; the civil servant was a man of expertise, not the creature of patronage of a century earlier.

To such administrators it had become clear by the late 1860s and 1870s just how intractable the problems facing the country had proved. Little had been achieved to solve the social ills of the time. Over the past 40 years the population had risen from 13.2 millions to 21.5 millions, natural increase being boosted by Irish immigration; this made things more difficult. In response the state began to intervene more fully and decisively.

Government purpose changed from negative to positive; from giving powers which others might use to imposition. The Artisans' and Labourers' Dwellings Act, 1868 – the first act of building legislation which overran the formerly sacred rights of private property – Forster's Education Act, 1870 and the Public Health Act,

1875 as well as the consolidating statutes of factory and mine reform all signalled a real shift towards a constructive programme. A. V. Dicey, writing in 1905 on 'Law and Public Opinion in England' labelled the years 1865–1900, the Period of Collectivism. Collectivism he defined as state action designed for the benefit of society as a whole, even at the expense of the sacrifice of some individual freedom.

However collectivism came into being – Dicey's ideas have been rigorously challenged – its development was encouraged by the moderation of working-class opinion. After the collapse of the GNCTU and Chartism, the lead in shaping working-class opinion was taken by the craft unions, the more privileged elements in Britain's workforce. They proved able to cooperate with both political parties setting the pattern for the British labour movement. Improvement rather than revolution was the aim; gaining the most that could be obtained within a capitalist society rather than Marxist ideals. British socialism in fact was collectivism. These trends were aided by the widening franchise achieved by the succession of Reform Acts. The result was the coming together of sensible, moderate democratic pressure and the constructive response of government.

From this fusion came further social reform and eventually the concept of the 'welfare state'. The machinery for the effective implementation of the new philosophy had also been created through the complete overhaul of local government: the creation of the county and county borough councils, the reorganisation of the boroughs and the development of urban and district councils. Local government was now able to range over a wide spread of activities from setting up public utilities to providing libraries and art galleries.

Under such stimuli much more change was achieved; there were still, however, what Churchill called the 'left-out millions'. Their plight was highlighted by the stresses in the British economy. The Liberal Administration, 1906–14 pioneered the founding of the welfare state. The Trade Boards Act, 1909, Old Age Pensions, 1908, Lloyd George's People's Budget, 1909, the Parliament Act, 1911 and the National Insurance Act of the same year helped to establish the principle that the wealth of the nation must be shared out more fairly and confirmed that further social reform was essential.

Of the new provisions that of insurance proved very important. Although the original scheme in time showed the need for modification, it still gave the stimulus necessary for expansion of the principle. The Act changed the relationship between employer and employee, between citizen and the state. The cost of this innovation was the future of the Liberal Party. Tasks of social reform developed more and more upon the Labour Party whose origins, close association with Liberalism, and connection with pragmatic trade unions ensured that further change would be guided by moderation and evolutionary ideas.

I The Problem Stated

Introduction

British society was not well equipped to deal with the problems that grew up in the early nineteenth century in the sense that there were no precedents to call upon. Peter Mathias, in his survey of the Industrial Revolution, made the point clearly by calling his book *The First Industrial Nation*. He wrote: 'the new industrial system, looked at from the point of view of standards of employment, the context of work, quickly broke up traditional patterns which had existed for centuries, as much as it created new problems. Living in industrial towns, the context of living rather than working, did create new and terrifying problems'. Nonetheless the great disorders which developed need to be seen in context. We cannot justly assess the nineteenth century by starting from our position today; comparison needs to be made with what went before. 'Any commentator has to remember the very poor standards existing before industrialising began' (Mathias). Caution is advisable in at least two ways if we are to avoid looking at nineteenth-century social conditions too negatively: the overall value of industrialisation and contemporary attitudes of people to one another.

Peter Mathias, in trying to emphasise the constructive view of industrialisation, has referred to Professor Ashton's book, *The Industrial Revolution*, the last paragraph of which he described as 'one of the most influential paragraphs in the writing of economic history in recent generations'. T. S. Ashton wrote:

The central problem of the age was how to feed and clothe and employ generations of children outnumbering by far those of any earlier time. Ireland was faced by the same problem. Failing to solve it, she lost in the 'forties about a fifth of her people by emigration or starvation or disease. If England had remained a nation of cultivators and craftsmen she could hardly have escaped the same fate, and, at the best, the weight of a growing population must have pressed down the spring of her spirit. She was delivered, not by her rulers, but by those who, seeking no doubt their own narrow ends, had the wit and resource to devise new methods of production and new methods of administering industry. There are today on the plains of India and China men and women, plague-ridden and hungry, living their lives little better, to outward appearance, than those of the cattle that toil with them by day and share their places of sleep by night. Such Asiatic standards, and such unmechanised horrors, are the lot of those who increase their numbers without passing through an industrial revolution.

Josiah Wedgwood, a true 'captain of industry' who imposed a strict working practice upon his workforce and rigorously supervised every aspect of manufacture at Etruria made the same point in the local context. In 'An Address to the Young Inhabitants of the Pottery', pp. 21–22 (quoted by P. Mantoux, *The Industrial Revolution in the Eighteenth Century*):

> I would request you to ask your parents for a description of the country we inhabit when they first knew it; and they will tell you that the inhabitants bore all the marks of poverty to a much greater degree than they do now. Their houses were miserable huts, the lands poorly cultivated and yielded little of value for the food of man or beast, and the disadvantages, with roads almost impassable, might be said to have cut off our part of the country from the rest of the world, besides rendering it not very comfortable to ourselves. Compare this picture which I know to be a true one, with the present state of the same country, the workmen earning near double their former wages, their houses mostly new and comfortable, and the lands, roads, and every other circumstance bearing evident marks of the most pleasing and rapid improvement. . . . Industry has been the parent of this happy change.

Secondly, contemporary standards of social judgement were frequently harsh, even perhaps, in our eyes, pitiless. Life was generally, as we should see it, brutalised. The prints of Hogarth vividly demonstrate the point as do the leisure pursuits of the time whether they were blood sports of considerable variety or an amused observation of the mental asylums or the spectacle of public hangings. The armed services were regulated by codes of extreme savagery while the common law sanctioned the death penalty for a bewildering range of offences. Not surprisingly then, contemporary attitudes to children were harsh. Long hours of employment were considered the best antidote to youthful vice. John Wesley in 1787 was greatly cheered by a silk mill which kept '250 children in perpetual employment'. Looking at life from a sternly moralist angle 'idleness was seen as the great abomination, the source of debauchery and beggary' (J. T. Ward, *The Factory Movement, 1830–1855*). Nathaniel Paterson, minister of Galashiels, asserted that 'there can be no training of the volatile minds of youth equal to that which is maintained in factories' (see Ward, above).

While industrialisation may have gone a long way to solving problems of large-scale poverty and starvation, and the tolerance of distress was high, it is also clear that industrialisation did create new forms of human misery. The point can be made by reference to child and female labour in factories. Mathias has described such toil as the 'bridge between the conditions of employment, in the old world of the putting-out system and the new factory world'. In the 'old world' child and female labour was part of 'family labour', where children worked under the supervision of, and jointly with, their parents. In the powered factory, however, the family unit broke down. Standards of discipline and work were devised and imposed not by parents but by the agents of the factory, the managers, the foremen, the supervisors. Women and all children, not merely the apprentices, came under a new and harsher code. In such a way were traditional relationships debased.

It was not only in the workplace that strains upon contemporary society were evident. Old towns such as London or Nottingham or Exeter had not been able to treat all the 'nuisances' from which they suffered. Population increase made things worse. In the newer, rapidly growing, centres of manufacture new and horrific problems developed. Industrial expansion resulted in the building of factories, housing, shops and so on; all this was done without regulation or perception of the need for it. Sanitation, drainage, water supply, street paving, lighting, road making, housing standards were the urban equivalents of long hours of work, industrial discipline, unregulated child and female labour, the provision of ventilation, sanitation and cooking facilities within the factories. Given the scale of change, truly a revolution in work practice and social conditions, it is hardly surprising that a multitude of new problems were created. Furthermore contemporary engineering could not easily solve the problems it had to meet; medical science was in its infancy; social science had scarcely been conceived in the modern sense. Prevention was impossible and remedies slow in coming.

Many of the difficulties then, which developed in industrialised Britain grew out of the very nature of the changes that took place. At the same time many people found themselves, like their agricultural forebears, under the direct exploitation of a few; of those 'few' some, like Robert Owen, were highly principled and humanitarian. Peter Mathias reminds us of others: 'Some of the apostles of laissez faire, who resisted every limitation imposed upon employers by statute in the name of individual liberty and the bogey of impending commercial disaster, deserved to end up on the lowest ledges of Dante's inferno. It is a false assumption that industrialisation had no tragedies or inequities to hide.'

1 Factory Rules

In some factories none but women are allowed to labour, excepting a few men, such as managers . . . not because the women can perform the work better or turn off a greater quantity, but because they are

considered to be more docile than men under the injustice that in
5 some shape or form is daily practised upon them.
   A great number of the females employed in factories are married,
and not a small number of them are mothers. It frequently happens
that the husband is refused work in the same mill with the wife;
under these circumstances the poor creature is obliged to leave her
10 husband in bed at five o'clock in the morning, while she hurries off
to the mill to undergo her daily repetition of drudgery, in order to
procure a scanty portion of food for her husband, herself, and her
helpless children. We have repeatedly seen married females, in the
last stage of pregnancy, slaving from morning till night beside these
15 never-tiring machines, and when oppressed nature became so
exhausted that they were obliged to sit down to take a moment's
ease, and being seen by the manager, were fined sixpence for the
offence. In some mills, the crime of sitting down to take a little rest is
visited with a penalty of one shilling, but let the masters and their
20 rules speak for themselves.
   1st. The door of the lodge will be closed ten minutes after the
engine starts every morning, and no weaver will afterwards be
admitted till breakfast-time. Any weaver who may be absent during
that time shall forfeit three-pence per loom.
25   2nd. Weavers absent at any other time when the engine is
working, will be charged three-pence per hour each loom for such
absence; and weavers leaving the room without the consent of the
overlooker, shall forfeit three-pence . . . .
   9th. All shuttles, brushes, oil-cans, wheels, windows, etc. if
30 broken, shall be paid for by the weaver.
   11th. If any hand in the mill is seen talking to another, whistling,
or singing, will be fined sixpence . . . .
   12th. For every rod broken, one penny will be stopped . . . .
   16th. For every wheel that breaks, from one shilling to two and
35 sixpence, according to size. Any weaver seen from his work during
mill-hours, will be fined sixpence . . . .

   Stubborn Facts from the Factories by a Manchester Operative,
   James Leach (published and dedicated to the working classes
   by William Rushleigh MP 1844), pp 11–15, quoted in
   E. Royston-Pike, *Human Documents of the Industrial
   Revolution* (Allen and Unwin, 1966)

Questions

a   What kind of behaviour is the factory owner trying to induce by
    Rule 1?
b   Why could it be claimed that Rule 2 was particularly unfeeling?
c   Why were Rules 9, 12 and 16 adopted?
d   Why should talking, whistling and singing be considered
    undesirable?

e What is the overall impression that these rules give?
f Why in some factories were only women employed (line 1)?
g What was there in the nature of factory work that made such rules possible and, for the factory owners, desirable?

2 'Truly infernal scenes'

Some of these lords of the loom have in their employ thousands of miserable creatures. In the cotton-spinning work, these creatures are kept, fourteen hours in each day, locked up, summer and winter, in a heat of from eighty to eighty-four degrees. The rules which they are
5 subjected to are such as no negroes were ever subjected to . . . .
Very seldom do we feel such a heat as this in England. The 31st of last August, and the 1st, 2nd and 3rd of last September, were very hot days. The newspapers told us that men had dropped down dead in the harvest fields, and that many horses had fallen dead upon the
10 road; and yet the heat during those days never exceeded eighty-four degrees in the hottest part of the day. We were retreating to the coolest rooms in our house; we were pulling off our coats, wiping the sweat off our faces, puffing, blowing, and panting, and yet we were living in a heat nothing like eighty degrees.
15 What, then, must be the situation of the poor creatures who are doomed to toil day after day, for three hundred and thirteen days in the year, fourteen hours in each day, in an average heat of eighty-two degrees? Can any man, with a heart in his body, and a tongue in his head, refrain from cursing a system that produces such slavery and
20 such cruelty?
Observe, too, that these poor creatures have no cool room to retreat to, not a moment to wipe off the sweat and not a breath of air to come and interpose itself between them and infection. The door of the place wherein they work, is locked, except half an hour, at
25 tea-time, the workpeople are not allowed to send for water to drink, in the hot factory; even the rain water is locked up, by the master's order, otherwise they would be happy to drink even that. If any spinner be found with his window open, he is to pay a fine of a shilling! Mr Martin, of Galway, has procured acts of parliament to
30 prevent cruelty to animals. If horses or dogs were shut up in a place like this, they would certainly be thought worthy of Mr Martin's attention.
Not only is there not a breath of sweet air in these truly infernal scenes, but, for a large part of the time, there is the abominable and
35 pernicious stink of the gas to assist in the murderous effects of the heat. In addition to the noxious effluvia of the gas, mixed with the steam, there are the dust, and what is called cotton-flyings or fuz, which the unfortunate creatures have to inhale; and the fact is, the notorious fact is, that well constitutioned men are rendered old and

40   past labour at forty years of age, and that children are rendered
decrepit and deformed, and thousands upon thousands of them
slaughtered by consumptions, before they arrive at the age of
sixteen . . . .
> William Cobbett, *Political Register*, vol LII, 20 Nov. 1824,
> quoted in E. Royston-Pike, op cit

Questions

a   What are the physical dangers that Cobbett thinks face the
factory worker?
b   What other dangers do they encounter?
c   What were the components of the 'noxious effluvia' (line 36);
how did they come to be present?
d   What is Cobbett's attitude to industrialisation?
★   e   Who was William Cobbett? What was his political significance?

3   Children in a Flax-Mill

Joseph Ward, fifteen years old, has worked in the preparing-room of
this mill for eight months. His father and three sisters work here. He
is tired in the evening, and often falls asleep at the work, as he
observes other boys and girls do. Is very anxious for short hours, and

5   think them at present such bondage, that 'they might as well be in a
prison' . . . . The overseer sometimes straps the boys for great
negligence. If the mill, owing to an accident, is stopped during the
day, the time is made up in the evening. He met with an accident by
having three of his fingers hurt by the machinery but was not

10   seriously injured.

     Christy Maclaren She frequently falls asleep at her work as all
young people do . . . . She met with an accident from the
machinery in the spinning-room, soon after she came, owing to her
ignorance and negligence and was obliged to have all of one of her

15   hands but the thumb amputated.

     Alexander Barr, fifteen years old, has been there for three years.
The long hours tire him, and make him sleepy in the evening, and
the dust or stour from the flax plagues his eyes, especially at the time
of the year when gas is used to light the mill . . . the dust in the mill is

20   sometimes like 'to choke him'.

     Mary Stodart She herself has a little girl at the mill, so tired
frequently that when she comes home she cares for nothing and
'stretches herself, and falls asleep, without tasting meat'.

     Andrew Pedie, twelve years old, has been three years in this mill.

25   *Joseph Dyer* He has a brother a ploughman, and a brother a
millwright, both stouter and healthier looking men than himself.
> Report of the Central Board: Factories Commission,
> *Parliamentary Papers*, 1833, Section A1, vol XX, pp 1–3

Questions

a What are the particular problems of a flax-mill which affect the working efficiency of the labour force?
b At what age did children begin to work in the mill?
c Which children were at most risk from industrial injury?
d Why was the child workforce relatively so unhealthy?
e What evidence is there in this extract of industrial discipline?

4 Industrial and Domestic Injury

The accidents which occur to the manufacturing population of Birmingham are very severe and numerous, as shown by the registers of the General Hospital. Many are the consequences of the want of proper attention to the fencing of machinery, which appears
5 to be seldom thought of in the manufactories, and many are caused by loose portions of dress being caught by the machinery, so as to drag the unfortunate sufferers under its power. The shawls of the females, or their long hair, and the aprons and loose sleeves of the boys and men, are in this way frequent causes of dreadful
10 mutilations.
One class of accidents is very frequent in Birmingham – severe burns and scalds. So numerous are these cases, particularly the former, that in the General Hospital two rooms are devoted to their reception . . . . A great number of these accidents we know to have
15 arisen from the children having been left without proper superintendence; and many are caused by the custom of wearing loose linen pinafores, which are drawn with the current of air into the fire.

Sanitary Conditions of the Labouring Population of England 1842
(Irish U.P. reprint), vol XXVII, p 208

Questions

a What were the main causes of industrial injury indicated by this extract?
b Why were the causes of industrial and domestic injuries so difficult to eradicate?
c What was the significance of the high incidence of injury for those who made clothes for the labouring classes?
★ *d* Examine the development in styles of dress during the nineteenth century.

5 Birmingham – healthier than most

The comparative exemption of Birmingham from the incursions of contagious disease was remarkably evinced during the prevalence of the Asiatic cholera in this country. In no town in the kingdom, in proportion to the amount of its population, were the ravages of cholera more terrible than at Bilston, which is situated only ten miles from Birmingham. Although the intercourse between the two places was uninterrupted, only 24 cases of cholera occurred in Birmingham during the year; and in the majority of these cases, it could be distinctly traced that the disease was imported, the patients having been affected with the early symptoms of cholera before they arrived in the town.

Perhaps it may be expected that we should state our opinion as to the causes which render fever comparatively so rare and so mild in Birmingham . . . . These are – the elevated situation of the town – its excellent natural drainage, and its abundant supply of water – the entire absence of cellars used as dwellings – the circumstance of almost every family having a separate house and lastly, the amount of wages received by the working classes, which may be regarded generally as adequate to procure the necessaries of life. Whatever depresses the vital powers appears to place the human body in a condition which is favourable to the attack of fever, or to render the disease more violent. Filth, an impure atmosphere, and putrid exhalations, by their depressing influence upon the vital energies, may produce these effects, or perhaps originate the disease; but in our opinion, anxiety of mind, penury, and starvation, and the depression of the bodily and mental powers which attends these conditions, are more frequent causes of fever than all the other sources to which it is attributed.

Ibid, p 859

Questions

a What are factors which this extract suggests caused cholera? Consider the possibility of both environmental and psychological factors.

b Which was the most potent cause of cholera in the view of those who conducted this investigation?

★ c What is the modern, scientific explanation of cholera and its rapid spread?

d Explain why the description of Birmingham in lines 14–19 contain the real explanation of the town's good fortune.

6 The Growth of Manchester

(a) The township of Manchester chiefly consists of dense masses of houses, inhabited by the population engaged in the great manufactories of the cotton trade. Some of the central divisions are occupied by warehouses and shops, and a few streets by the

5   dwellings of some of the more wealthy inhabitants; but the opulent
merchants chiefly reside in the country, and even the superior
servants of their establishments inhabit the suburban townships.
Manchester, properly so called, is chiefly inhabited by shopkeepers
and the labouring classes. These districts where the poor dwell are of
10   very recent origin. The rapid growth of the cotton manufacture has
attracted hither operatives from every part of the kingdom, and
Ireland has poured forth the most destitute of her hordes to supply
the constantly increasing demand for labour. This immigration has
been . . . a serious evil.
     J. P. Kay, *The Moral and Physical Condition of the Working
Classes employed in the cotton manufacture in Manchester* (E. J.
Morton, Manchester impression, 1969), pp 20–21

15   (b) The Irk, black with the refuse of Dye-works erected on its
banks, receives excrementitious matters from some sewers in this
portion of the town – the drainage from the gas-works, and filth of
the most pernicious character from bone-works, tanneries, size
manufactories . . . . The parish burial ground occupies one side of
20   the stream, and a series of courts of the most singular and unhealthy
character, the other . . . . One nuisance frequently occurs in these
districts . . . . The houses of the poor sometimes surround a
common area, into which the doors and windows open at the back of
the dwelling.
25   Porkers, who feed pigs in the town, often contract with the
inhabitants to pay some small sum for the rent of their area, which is
immediately covered with pigstyes, and converted into a dung-heap
and receptacle of the putrescent garbage, upon which the animals are
fed, as also the refuse which is now heedlessly flung into it from all
30   the surrounding dwellings . . . . There is no Common Slaughter-
house in Manchester, and those which exist are chiefly situated in the
narrowest and most filthy streets in the town. The drainage from
these houses, deeply tinged with blood, and impregnated with other
animal matters, frequently flows down the common surface drain of
35   the street, and stagnates in the ruts and pools.
     J. P. Kay, ibid, pp 38–9

Questions

a   What evidence do these extracts give to explain the way in which
     Manchester developed?
b   What contributed to the pollution of the Irk?
c   Why was the Irk's condition so important?
d   Under the conditions described in the extracts, what would you
     have considered the most likely methods of the transmission of
     disease?

e Why did these conditions threaten the health of even the 'opulent merchants' and their 'superior servants' (lines 5–7)?
f What kind of builder probably put up the houses of the working population?

7   A Small Town in the Country

In Tiverton there is a large district, from which I find numerous applications were made for relief to the Board of Guardians, in consequence of illness from fever . . . . The district is nearly on a level with the water; the ground is marshy and the sewers all open.
5   Before reaching the district, I was assailed by a most disagreeable smell; and it was clear to the sense that the air was full of the most injurious malaria. The inhabitants, easily distinguishable from the inhabitants from the other part of the town, had all a sickly, miserable appearance. The open drains in some cases ran
10   immediately before the doors of the houses, and some of the houses were surrounded by wide open drains, full of all the animal and vegetable refuse not only of the houses in that part, but of those in other parts of Tiverton.

A. D. Acland, *Sanitary Conditions of the Labouring Population of England, 1842*, vol XXVII, The Counties of Devon and Cornwall (Irish U.P. reprint), p 640

Questions

a Where is Tiverton?
b Was it an industrial town?
c What were the 'Board of Guardians' (line 2)?
d What is meant by the 'most injurious malaria' (lines 6–7)?
e Why did so many of those living in the low-lying district in Tiverton have 'a sickly, miserable appearance' (lines 8–9)?

8   Life of the Working Classes in the Countryside

The accommodation in the cottages in the poorer classes is very insufficient in many respects, according to our views of what is necessary. It does not appear that the poor themselves feel it to be at all an inconvenience, or not generally so. It is in their moral habits
5   that the evil is mostly seen.

With regard to their moral habits as connected with their cottages, there is one very great and serious evil – the growing of brothers and sisters to years of puberty in the same bedrooms with their married parents, and even with a married brother-in-law and sister, or the
10   converse. By this means it is obvious that the habits of indelicate thought and conversation, and ultimately of action, are soon

produced. In fact few women in this neighbourhood ever marry until they have had, or show obvious signs of being about to have, their first infant. I am far from saying that their greater separation would secure morality; that security is to be found in higher powers, and in principles inculcated by early religious education, and careful superintendence; but their mode of life does tend to undermine their existence, even where those principles are implanted, and affords a ready stimulus to evil where that has commenced.

Ibid, p 645

Questions

a Why did such intense overcrowding lead to 'habits of indelicate thought and conversation, and ultimately of action' (lines 10–11)?

b What did Acland consider were the solutions to the problem of extra-marital pregnancies? What did he mean by 'higher powers' and 'careful superintendence' (lines 15–17)?

c What does this extract tell you of the outlook of this member of a highly distinguished local family?

9 'It's a knife and fork question'

(a) The population employed in the cotton factories rises at five o'clock in the morning, works in the mills from six to eight o'clock, and returns home for half an hour or forty minutes to breakfast. This meal generally consists of tea or coffee, with a little bread. Oatmeal porridge is sometimes, but of late rarely used, and chiefly by the men; but the stimulus of tea is preferred, and especially by the women. The tea is almost always of a bad, and sometimes of a deleterious quality; the infusion is weak, and little or no milk is added. The operatives return to the mills and workshops until twelve o'clock, when an hour is allowed for dinner. Amongst those who obtain the lower rate of wages this meal generally consists of boiled potatoes. The mess of potatoes is put into one large dish; melted lard and butter are poured upon them, and a few pieces of fried fat bacon are sometimes mingled with them, and but seldom a little meat. Those who obtain better wages, or families whose aggregate income is larger, add a greater proportion of animal food to this meal, at least three times in the week; but the quantity consumed by the labouring population is not great. The family sit around the table, and each rapidly appropriates his portion on a plate, or they all plunge their spoons into the dish, and with an animal eagerness satisfy the cravings of their appetite. At the expiration of the hour, they are again employed in the workshops or mills, where they continue until seven o'clock or a later hour, when

they generally indulge in the use of tea, often mingled with spirits
25 accompanied by a little bread. Oatmeal or potatoes are however
taken by some a second time in the evening. The comparatively
innutritious qualities of these articles of diet are most evident.
J. P. Kay, op cit, pp 23–4

(b) A cotton spinner's budget, 1835:
The weekly earnings were twenty-five shillings and 75 per cent of
30 the wages were spent on necessaries.

1½ lbs butter	1s.3d
1½ ozs tea	4½d
Bread baked at home	4s.6d
½ peck oatmeal	6½d
35 1½ lbs bacon	9d
40 lbs potatoes	1s.4d
7 quarts milk	1s.9d
1 lb meat on Sunday	7d
1½ lb sugar	9d
40 Pepper salt etc.	3d
Soap and candles	1s.0d
Coals	1s.6d
Rent	3s.6d
Total	18s.1d

Balance remaining for education, clothes, sickness etc. 6s.11d.
Factory Inquiry Commission 1st Report, Section D, 1833
(London, 1834), quoted in J. Addy, *The Textile Revolution*
(Longman Seminar Series, 1976)

Questions

a What are the main elements in the diet of these industrial
workers?
b Do you think they had a 'balanced' diet?
★ c Was this diet suitable for a family of factory workers?
d Were there any deficiencies in this diet? If so, how did they affect
people?
e Does Dr Kay indicate any reason to conclude that large families
were encouraged by low wages?

10   Trapping in the Mine

It is almost superfluous to state, that on the proper ventilation of air
the lives of the miners depend. The ventilation again depends
entirely on the trap-doors being kept shut and on their being

properly closed immediately after the carriages conveying the coal
5 have passed them.

The youngest children in the mines are intrusted with this
important office. They are called trappers. Their duty consists in
sitting in a little hole, scooped out for them in the side of the gates
behind each door, where they sit with a string in their hands attached
10 to the door, and pull it the moment they hear the corves (i.e. the
carriages for conveying the coal) at hand, and the moment it has
passed they let the door fall to, which it does of its own weight. If
anything impedes the shutting of the door they remove it, or, if
unable to do so, run to the nearest man to do it for them. They have
15 nothing else to do; but, as their office must be performed from the
repassing of the first to the passing of the last corve during the day,
they are in the pit the whole time it is worked, frequently about 12
hours a day. They sit, moreover, in the dark, often with a damp floor
to stand on, and exposed necessarily to drafts, though I have seldom
20 found the temperature lower at their posts than 58°, and often
higher.

The ages of these children vary from 5½ to 10 years old; few come
before they are nearly seven, and few remain longer than 9 to 10.
There is no hard work for these children to do, – nothing can be
25 easier; but it is a most painful thing to contemplate the dull
dungeon-like life these little creatures are doomed to spend; a life, for
the most part, passed in solitude, damp, and darkness. They are
allowed no light; but sometimes a good-natured collier will bestow a
little bit of candle on them as a treat.

Parliamentary Papers, 1842, vol XVI, p 174, quoted in
E. Royston-Pike, op cit

Questions

a Can you suggest why such young children were employed for
the job of trapping?
b What physical dangers did they face?
c Is there some justification for saying that the main pressures upon
the children were psychological?
d Explain why ventilation 'depends entirely on the trap-doors
being kept shut' (lines 2–3).
e Does this extract help to explain some of the causes of mining
accidents?

11 'Very hard work for a woman'

Betty Harris, age 37: I was married at 23, and went into a colliery
when I was married. I used to weave when about 12 years old; can
neither read nor write. I work for Andrew Knowles, of Little Bolton
(Lancs), and make sometimes 7s a week, sometimes not so much. I

5   am a drawer, and work from 6 in the morning to 6 at night. Stop
     about an hour at noon to eat my dinner; have bread and butter for
     dinner; I get no drink. I have two children, but they are too young to
     work. I worked at drawing when I was in the family way. I know a
     woman who has gone home and washed herself, taken to her bed,
10   been delivered of a child, and gone to work again under the week.
          I have a belt round my waist, and a chain passing between my legs,
     and I go on my hands and feet. The road is very steep, and we have to
     hold by a rope; and when there is no rope, by anything we can catch
     hold of. There are six women and about six boys and girls in the pit I
15   work in; it is very hard work for a woman. The pit is very wet where
     I work, and the water comes over our clog-tops always, and I have
     seen it up to my thighs; it rains in at the roof terribly. My clothes are
     wet through almost all day long. I never was ill in my life, but when I
     was lying in.
20   My cousin looks after my children in the day time. I am very tired
     when I get home at night; I fall asleep sometimes before I get washed.
          Patience Kershaw, age 17, Halifax: I go to pit at 5 o'clock in the
     morning and come out at 5 in the evening; I get my breakfast,
     porridge and milk, first; I take my dinner with me, a cake, and eat it
25   as I go; I do not stop or rest at any time for the purpose, I get nothing
     else until I get home, and then have potatoes and meat, not every day
     meat.
          I hurry in the clothes I have now got on – trousers and a ragged
     jacket; the bald place upon my head is made by thrusting the corves; I
30   hurry the corves a mile and more under ground and back; they weigh
     3 cwt. I hurry eleven a day. I wear a belt and chain at the workings to
     get the corves out. The getters that I work for are naked except their
     caps; they pull off all their clothes; I see them at work when I go up.
          Sometimes they beat me if I am not quick enough, with their
35   hands; they strike me upon my back. The boys take liberties with me
     sometimes; they pull me about. I am the only girl in the pit; there are
     about 20 boys and 15 men; all the men are naked. I would rather
     work in mill than in coal-pit.
          Note by Sub-Commissioner Scriven: This girl is an ignorant,
40   filthy, ragged, and deplorable looking object, and such a one as the
     uncivilized natives of the prairies would be shocked to look upon.
          Parliamentary Papers, 1842, vol XVII, p 108, quoted in
          E. Royston-Pike, op cit

Questions

a   Why was drawing such 'very hard work for a woman' (line 15)?
b   What dangers to health does this extract reveal?
c   What moral dangers did young women face in the mines?
d   Can you think of any reason why Patience Kershaw preferred
     work in the mill to that in the coal-pit (line 38)?

12 'He finds me in victuals and drink'

Thomas Moorhouse, a collier boy: I don't know how old I am; father is
dead; I am a chance child; mother is dead also; I don't know how long
she has been dead; 'tis better na three years.

5   I began to hurry when I was 9 years old for William Greenwood; I
was apprenticed to him till I should be 21 . . . . The overseers gave
him a sovereign to buy clothes with, but he never laid it out; I ran
away from him because he lost my indentures, for he served me very
bad; he struck a pick into me twice in my bottom. (Here I made the
boy strip, and I found a large cicatrix likely to have been occasioned
10 by such an instrument . . . . There were twenty other wounds,
occasioned by hurrying in low workings . . . .) He used to hit me
with the belt, and mawl or sledge, and fling coals at me; he served me
so bad that I left him, and went about to see if I could get a job.

I used to sleep in the cabins upon the pit's bank, and in the old pits
15 that had done working; I laid upon the shale all night; I used to get
what I could to eat; I eat for a long time the candles that I found in the
pits that the colliers left over night; I had nothing else to eat . . . .
When I got out next morning, I looked about for work, and begged
of the people a bit. I got to Bradford after a while . . . . I work now
20 here for John Cawtherly; he took me into his house, and is serving
me well; I hurry for him now, and he finds me in victuals and drink.

Mr Scriven's report, *Parliamentary Papers*, 1842, vol XV,
p 43, quoted in E. Royston-Pike, op cit

Questions

a   Within the mine the drawers took on apprentices to hurry (i.e.
move coals) for them. What kind of treatment did this boy
experience from his master?
b   Why was such a boy even more vulnerable to exploitation than
other children?
c   Who were the 'overseers' (line 5)?
d   Why was William Greenwood given a sovereign (line 6)?
e   What were 'indentures' (line 7)?
f   How does this boy's experience reflect upon the operation of the
Poor Law Amendment Act?

II Ideas, Beliefs and Principles

Laissez faire and State Intervention

S. E. Finer, in his biography of Sir Edwin Chadwick, noted the importance of the political economists of the early nineteenth century: 'They were the only people who had studied legislation as a science. They followed up topics in the daily press, they collected statistics, and formed reasoned conclusions. They were the amateur professionals in an age which boasted only amateurs. Compared with the Cabinets they not infrequently advised, they were authorities.' From their work emerged the *laissez faire* philosophy; among the leaders were David Ricardo, J. R. McCulloch and Nassau Senior. They developed the economic analysis stimulated by Adam Smith. Harmonising as it did with the entrepreneurial spirit of the time, this philosophy became one of the most dominant sources of ideas and the most powerful of influences.

For the political economists the opinions of the Reverend Thomas Malthus acted as a powerful reinforcement. He held that all private charity and government action could not, separately or jointly, solve the problem of the unemployed and the poor; indeed they seemed to worsen the situation. Not surprisingly, his pessimistic outlook helped to earn for political economy the tag of the 'dismal science'. Such ideas contrasted with the optimism of Jeremy Bentham, who believed that through his energy and rational faculties, man could improve his position.

Bentham took a very different line from the earlier philosophers; whereas they were much concerned with the origins and structures of government, he was interested in assessing the value of government, its ability to promote the well-being of society. The art of government consisted in legislating to ensure the greatest happiness of the greatest number of individuals; government should aim to increase the sum of welfare, though there was a limit to what the legislator could do. The law-maker could not know more of the interest of the individual than the individual himself.

There were few advocates of the complete *laissez faire* principle, which Thomas Carlyle, Charles Dickens and Charles Kingsley attacked so vigorously. Indeed Adam Smith, who has been popularly regarded as the supreme apologist of free-trade capitalism, had much broader concerns. As a philosopher of the Enlightenment, he was interested in freeing men from the restrictions of arbitrary, unrepresentative government. Thus his views upon economic liberalism formed part of a much wider concept. His commitment to *laissez faire* was less than total. 'As defence,' he said, 'is of much more importance than opulence, the act of navigation is, perhaps, the wisest of all the commercial regulations of England.'

Radicals, like John Bright and Richard Cobden, who led the 'Manchester School', insisted upon the complete freedom of economic enterprise. On the other hand, Edwin Chadwick took the view that where private interest prevented the achievement of the greatest public interest, it might have to be removed. He used state power to remove those things which stood in the way of free competition, profitability, and individualism, as in reorganising the Poor Law. Behind the colossal figure of Chadwick was a growing army of 'experts', doctors, statisticians and civil servants, among whom can be numbered the new government inspectors. It was in part due to the efforts of men like Sir James Kay-Shuttleworth (formerly Dr J. P. Kay), Dr Thomas Southwood Smith, William Farr, the first Registrar General, and the Factory Inspector Leonard Horner, that reform was achieved. Equally important, however, were the humanitarians who, often actively, opposed the new political economy.

'Richard Oastler, a land agent, Michael Sadler, a linen merchant, and the Reverend George Bull, an evangelical curate, all from the West Riding of Yorkshire, were Tory paternalists. They were sceptical of the benefits presumed to flow from unfettered competition and they saw the state as the natural agency whereby the most brutish aspects of industrial capitalism could be curbed . . . . The Parliamentary leadership of the factory reformers devolved onto Lord Ashley' (E. J. Evans, *The Forging of the Modern State, 1783–1870*, Longman, 1983)

1 Self-Help: National and Individual

'Heaven helps those who help themselves' is a well-tried maxim, embodying in a small compass the results of vast human experience. The spirit of self-help is the root of all genuine growth in the individual; and, exhibited in the lives of many, it constitutes the true
5   source of national vigour and strength. Help from without is often enfeebling in its effects, but help from within invariably invigorates. Whatever is done for men or classes, to a certain extent takes away the stimulus and necessity of doing for themselves; and where men are subjected to over-guidance and over-government, the inevitable
10   tendency is to render them comparatively helpless.

Even the best institutions can give a man no active help. Perhaps

the most they can do is to leave him free to develop himself and improve his individual condition. But in all times men have been prone to believe that their happiness and well-being were to be
15 secured by means of institutions rather than by their own conduct. Hence the value of legislation as an agent in human advancement has usually been much over-estimated. To constitute the millionth part of a Legislature, by voting for one or two men once in three or five years, however conscientiously this duty may be performed, can
20 exercise but little active influence upon any man's life and character. Moreover, it is every day becoming more clearly understood that the function of Government is negative and restrictive, rather than positive and active; being resolvable principally into protection – protection of life, liberty and property. Laws, wisely administered,
25 will secure men in the enjoyment of the fruits of their labour, whether of mind or body, at a comparatively small personal sacrifice; but no laws, however stringent, can make the idle industrious, the thriftless provident, or the drunken sober. Such reforms can only be effected by means of individual action,
30 economy, and self-denial, by better habits, rather than by greater rights.

> Samuel Smiles, *Self-Help* (revised edn 1866, Centenary Reprint, John Murray, 1958), pp 35–6

Questions

a Do you agree that '[h]elp from without is often enfeebling in its effects' (lines 5–6)?

b Do 'over-guidance and over-government' leave people 'comparatively helpless' (lines 9–10)?

c What are the best kinds of institutions of government in the opinion of Samuel Smiles?

d Why does Samuel Smiles consider that the individual does not find himself the focus of concern in representative institutions of government?

e What are the limits of government influence?

f Of what types of nineteenth-century citizen was Samuel Smiles characteristic?

2 Private Initiative and Public Benefit

As every individual, therefore, endeavours as much as he can both to employ his capital in the support of domestic industry, and so to direct that industry that its produce may be of the greatest value; every individual necessarily labours to render the annual revenue of
5 the society as great as he can. He generally, indeed, neither intends to promote the public interest, nor knows how much he is promoting it. By preferring the support of domestic to that of foreign industry,

he intends only his own security; and by directing that industry in
such a manner as its produce may be of the greatest value, he intends
10 only his own gain, and he is in this, as in many other cases, led by an
invisible hand to promote an end which was no part of his intention.
Nor is it always the worse for the society that it was no part of it. By
pursuing his own interest he frequently promotes that of the society
more effectually than when he really intends to promote it. I have
15 never known much good done by those who affected to trade for the
public good.
    Adam Smith, *The Wealth of Nations* (Everyman edn, Dent,
    1910), vol I, p 400

Questions

a Explain how Smith considers the actions of the individual can
    benefit the whole community.
b How do you think Smith regarded state restriction of the
    economic freedom of the individual?
c Are there any disadvantages to unrestrained individual freedom?
★ *d* What do you know of the career and importance of Adam Smith?

3 'A System of Unrestricted Freedom'

Instead, then, of any longer contenting ourselves and soothing our
consciences with idly nibbling at the outskirts of a vast and growing
mischief in our social state, – let us have the courage and candour to
go at once to the origin of the evil – to strike at the source of that
5 malady which has so long withered up the physical energies and
moral virtues of our people. Let us unfetter the springs of the
national industry, in the full confidence that, if we do so, it has an
expansive elasticity within it, sufficient to absorb into profitable
employment all those numbers whom it is now the fashion to
10 consider as redundant. That, under a system of unrestricted
freedom, the field of employment is capable of this indefinite
enlargement, is the conviction of all the best informed of our
Practical Economists; – and few who differ from this opinion will
allow, that the colonization to which they look as a subsidiary relief,
15 will be most safely and beneficially conducted, when left to the
operation of natural motives of an intelligent and instructed people.
    Edinburgh Review, vol 79, 1844, pp 130–56, quoted in *British
    Labour Struggles, Contemporary Pamphlets, 1720–1850* (New
    York, Anno Press, 1972)

Questions

a What does the Review mean when it says: 'Let us unfetter the
    springs of the national industry' (lines 6–7)?

b How did the Review consider full employment could be assured (lines 8–10)?
c Who were the 'Practical Economists' (line 13)?
d What was the 'malady' which restricted British prosperity (line 5)?
★ *e* What course of action did the Review demand the British government should take?
★ *f* Was the Review's advice followed?

4 'Letting Alone'

Letting alone should be the general practice: every departure from it, unless required by some great good, is a certain evil.

We have observed that, as a general rule, the business of life is better performed when those who have an immediate interest in it
5 are left to take their own course, uncontrolled either by the mandate of the law or by the meddling of any public functionary. The persons, or some of the persons, who do the work, are likely to be better judges than the government, of the means of attaining the particular end at which they aim. Were we to suppose, what is not
10 very probable, that the government has possessed itself of the best knowledge which had been acquired up to a given time by the persons most skilled in the occupation; even then, the individual agents have so much stronger and more direct an interest in the result, that the means are far more likely to be improved and
15 perfected if left to their uncontrolled choice. But if the workman is generally the best selector of means, can it be affirmed with the same universality that the consumer, or person served, is the most competent judge of the end? Is the buyer always qualified to judge of the commodity? If not, the presumption in favour of the
20 competition of the market does not apply to the case; and if the commodity be one, in the quality of which society has much at stake, the balance of advantages may be in favour of some mode and degree of intervention, by the authorised representatives of the collective interest of the state.
25 Education . . . is one of those things which it is admissible in principle that a government should provide for the people. The case is one to which the reasons of the non-interference principle do not necessarily or universally extend . . . . In the matter of education, the intervention of government is justifiable, because the case is not
30 one in which the interest and judgment of the consumer are a sufficient security for the goodness of the commodity . . . .

The maxim is unquestionably sound as a general rule; but there is no difficulty in perceiving some very large and conspicuous exceptions to it.

J. S. Mill, *Principles of Political Economy* (1848, reprint of 6th edn, Longman, 1909), pp 573–7

Questions

a What does John Stuart Mill mean when he says, 'letting alone should be the general practice' (line 1)?

b Explain what is meant by 'the mandate of the law' and the 'meddling of any public functionary' (lines 5–6)?

c Are the people 'who do the work' (line 7) likely to be the best judges of what they ought to do?

★ d Were governments of the mid–nineteenth century likely to know little that would benefit the businessman (lines 9–12)?

e Do you agree with Mill's views on education? Doesn't 'the customer know best'? (Bear in mind the educational provision of the time.)

f How far did Mill qualify his belief in *laissez faire*?

5 The Principle of Population

Taking the population of the world at any number, a thousand millions for instance, the human species would increase in the ratio of – 1, 2, 4, 8, 16, 32, 64, 128, 256, 512 etc. and subsistence as – 1, 2, 3, 4, 5, 6, 7, 8, 9, 10 etc. In two centuries and a quarter, the population
5   would be to the means of subsistence as 512 to 10: in three centuries as 4096 to 13; and in two thousand years the difference would be almost incalculable, though the produce in that time would have increased to an immense extent.

No limits whatever are placed to the productions of the earth; they
10   may increase for ever and be greater than any assignable quantity; yet still the power of population being a power of a superior order, the increase of the human species can only be kept commensurate to the increase in the means of subsistence, by the constant operation of the strong law of necessity acting as a check upon the greater
15   power . . . .

The food therefore which before supported seven millions, must now be divided among seven millions and a half or eight millions. The poor consequently must live much worse, and many of them be reduced to severe distress. The number of labourers also being above
20   the proportion of the work in the market, the price of labour must tend toward a decrease; while the price of provisions would at the same time tend to rise. The labourer therefore must work harder to earn the same as he did before. During this season of distress, the discouragements to marriage, and the difficulty of rearing a family
25   are so great, that population is at a stand. In the meantime the cheapness of labour, the plenty of labourers, and the necessity of an increased industry amongst them encourage cultivators to employ more labour upon their land . . . till ultimately the means of

subsistence become in the same proportion to the population as at
30   the period from which we set out.

Reverend Thomas Malthus, *An Essay on the Principle of
Population* (1798, facsimile reprint, Macmillan, 1966), pp 25–6,
30–31

Questions

a   In what kind of ratios did Malthus think population and food
production would increase (lines 3–4)?
b   Explain what is meant by 'the power of population being a power
of a superior order' (line 11).
c   Why would the price of food tend to rise and wages tend to fall
(lines 20–22)?
d   What problems were disguised by the expression 'the difficulty
of rearing a family' (line 24)?
e   What type of birth control does Malthus identify?
f   Malthus thought it unlikely that there could ever be a 'great
permanent amelioration' of the condition of the poor; has he
proved his case?
★   g   What do you know of the career and importance of Malthus? Did
his work deserve to be known as part of the 'dismal science' of
political economy?

6   'The greatest happiness of the greatest number'

Nature has placed mankind under the governance of two sovereign
masters, pain and pleasure. It is for them alone to point out what we
ought to do, as well as to determine what we shall do. On the one
hand the standard of right and wrong, on the other the chain of
5   causes and effects, are fastened on their throne. They govern us in all
we do, in all we say, in all we think: every effort we can make to
throw off our subjection, will serve but to demonstrate and confirm
it . . . . The *principle of utility* recognises this subjection, and
assumes it for the foundation of that system, the object of which is to
10   rear the fabric of felicity by the hands of reason and labour . . . . By
the principle of utility is meant that principle which approves or
disapproves of every action whatsoever, according to the tendency
which it appears to have to augment or diminish the happiness of the
party whose interest is in question . . . not only of every action of a
15   private individual, but of every measure of government.

The interest of the community then is, what? – the sum of the
interests of the several members who compose it. It is vain to talk of
the interest of the community, without understanding what is the
interest of the individual. A thing is said to promote the interest, or
20   to be *for* the interest of an individual, when it tends to add to the sum
total of his pleasures. The happiness of the individuals, of whom a

community is composed, that is their pleasures and their security, is the end and the sole end which the legislator ought to have in view.

Jeremy Bentham, *An Introduction to the Principles of Morals and Legislation*, ed. Harrison (Blackwell, 1967), pp 125–47

Questions

a What, in Bentham's view, is the law of Nature that shapes our actions (lines 1–2)?

b What is the *'principle of utility'* (line 8)?

c By what means can men and women shape their own happiness (lines 9–10)?

d Does Bentham think that governments are affected by the *'principle of utility'*? If so, how are governments influenced?

e How does Bentham interpret 'community' (lines 16–17)? Why does he look at the word in this way? Are alternative interpretations possible?

f What is the 'interest of the community' (line 18)? Does everyone benefit from its improvement?

g What is the 'sole end' of government (line 23)?

7 Central Power and Uniform Provision

We trust that immediate measures for the correction of the evils in question may be carried into effect by a comparatively small and cheap agency, which may assist the parochial or district officers, wherever their management is in conformity with the legislature;
5 and control them whenever their management is at variance with it . . . .

The course of proceeding which we recommend for adoption, is in principle that which the legislature adopted for the management of the savings banks, the friendly societies etc. Having prescribed the
10 outline and general principles on which those institutions should be conducted, a special agency . . . was appointed to see that their rules and detailed regulations conformed to the intentions of the law. This agency, we believe, has accomplished the object effectively.

We recommend, therefore, the appointment of a Central Board to
15 control the administration of the Poor Laws . . . and that the Commissioners be empowered and directed to frame and enforce regulations for the government of workhouses . . . and that such regulations shall be uniform throughout the country . . . .

Edwin Chadwick, *Poor Law Report, 1834* (HMSO reprint, 1905), p 297

Questions

a What did Chadwick mean by 'a comparatively small and cheap agency' (lines 2–3)?

★   *b*   Why did Chadwick insist upon economy of administration (lines 2–3)?

      c   What was to be the function of the government administration (lines 3–6)?

      d   Upon what legislative arrangements did Chadwick want to base the administration of the Poor Law (lines 7–13)?

      e   Why did Chadwick insist that a Central Board was needed (line 14)?

★   *f*   What virtue did Chadwick see in uniform regulations?

      g   Why did Chadwick consider the Poor Law to be a necessary evil?

8   'There is no time to be lost'

We have some reason to be gratified by the appearance of Mr Horner's pamphlet (On the Employment of Children in Factories and other Works etc.). While it shows many imperfections of detail, it affirms the success of mercy by Statute; and declares, on a
5   retrospect of the last seven years, the commencement of many of those great and good results which we were called fools and zealots for venturing to prophesy. We do recollect the clamour: the awful predictions of a ruined trade and a starving population; commerce flying to foreign shores; England depressed; France exalted in the
10   scale of nations.

     We had one great and quickening principle, comfortable and true as revelation itself (for it was deduced from it), that nothing which is morally wrong can be politically right.

     The two great demons in morals and politics, Socialism and
15   Chartism, are stalking through the land; yet they are but the symptoms of an universal disease, spread throughout vast masses of the people, who, so far from concurring in the status quo suppose anything better than their present condition . . . . No wonder that thousands of hearts should be against a system which establishes the
20   relations, without calling forth the mutual sympathies, of master and servant, landlord and tenant, employer and employed . . . the rich and the poor are antagonist parties, each watching for the opportunities to gain an advantage over the other.

     But here comes the worst of all these vast multitudes, ignorant and
25   excitable in themselves, and rendered still more so by oppression or neglect, are surrendered, almost without a struggle, to the experimental philosophy of infidels and democrats. When called upon to suggest our remedy to the evil, we reply by an exhibition of the causes of it; the very statement involves an argument, and
30   contains its own answer within itself. Let your laws, we say to Parliament, assume the proper functions of law, protect those for whom neither wealth, nor station, nor age, have raised a bulwark against tyranny; but above all, open your treasury, erect churches, send forth the ministers of religion; reverse the conduct of the enemy

35 of mankind, and sow wheat among the tares – all hopes are
groundless, all legislation weak, all conservatism nonsense, without
this alpha and omega of policy; it will give content instead of
bitterness, engraft obedience on rebellion, raise purity from
corruption, and life from the dead – but there is no time to be lost.
Earl of Shaftesbury in the *Quarterly Review*, 1849, vol 67,
pp 171–81, reprinted in J. Saville, *Working Conditions in the
Victorian Age* (Farnborough, 1973)

Questions

a Who was Mr Horner (lines 1–2)?
b What is meant by 'mercy by Statute' (line 4)? To what Statute is
   Shaftesbury referring?
c Who made the predictions of ruined trade and other disasters
   (line 8)? (See Chapter 3.)
d To what 'revelation' is Shaftesbury making reference (line 12)?
e What 'system' did the masses of the people resent (line 19)?
f Why was that system failing in its responsibilities (lines 18–23)?
g What was the 'experimental philosophy of infidels and
   democrats' (line 27)?
h How does Shaftesbury view parliament's function (lines 30–39)?
★ i How far does this extract exemplify Shaftesbury's beliefs?

9 'Tory "live and let live" principles'

Machinery, which was intended to be a blessing to the labourer, by
decreasing the severity of his toil, and *shortening* the hours of his
labour, is his greatest curse, – and why? – because the capitalist has
been enabled to erect large mills or factories, – to fill them with
5   untaxed machinery, – and to bring thousands into those mills to
work at machines *which are not their own*. They consequently have to
labour, not only for themselves, but to pay the interest of the
expensive establishments of their masters, and an immense profit to
satisfy the avaricious demands of the proprietors. Thus they have to
10 work *longer* hours than when they were employed at home, with less
perfect machinery. Nay more, the bodily ease which machinery was
intended to give to the working man, has, in tens of thousands of
cases, thrown him entirely out of employment, – his children,
having to labour from twelve to eighteen hours a day; whilst he
15 subsists, unwillingly, in idleness, on the fruits of their excessive toil.
The tens of thousands of adult labourers, who are thus thrown out of
work, naturally become dissatisfied; listen to the harangues against
the landed interest; and are persuaded to believe, that the owners of
the soil, are their bitterest enemies.
20   The political economist then whispers to the aristocrats, 'You had

better get rid of them': and the government is so infatuated as to spend immense sums of money annually, in transporting the flower of the British nation, to far distant climes . . . .

25 This state of things cannot long continue. The poor only want bread for their labour, and they deserve it. They are not disloyal, – no man can know their feelings better than myself. They absolutely hate the Whigs; and if the Tories would act upon true Tory 'live and let live' principles, the people would, I am sure, rally round them, and the country might be saved.

Letter of Richard Oastler to the Duke of Wellington, 24 July 1832, quoted in *British Labour Struggles*

Questions

a   Why has machinery become the labourer's 'greatest curse' (line 3)?
b   If machinery had been taxed, for whose benefit could the income have been used (line 5)?
c   Who has tried to turn the working people against the 'landed interest' (line 18)?
★ d   To what evidence could factory owners point to suggest that landowners were oppressing the poor?
e   How did the 'political economist' (line 20) recommend the government to deal with the unemployed?
f   Why did the factory workers hate the Whigs (lines 26–7)?
★ g   Why was Oastler writing to the Duke of Wellington?

III Factory Reform: Conditions

Introduction

It was not an easy task to bring parliament to legislate on the factories or on the other problems which were generated by industrialisation or by the inheritance from past generations of town dwellers. The legislature became the focus of a vast amount of propaganda which explained the vices and virtues of the textile factories, which pointed out the dire consequences of parliamentary intervention, which claimed that inaction would bring equally unfortunate results. Indeed the very principle of parliament acting at all upon such issues was in dispute. Althorp, in explaining his proposals in 1833, said that he still entertained doubts on the propriety of the legislature's interfering between master and servant. Nonetheless, he admitted that if children were placed in a situation in which they could not protect themselves, it was the duty of the House of Commons to afford protection to them.

The evidence brought forward before an increasingly scandalised national conscience seemed contradictory. Some witnesses urged that big factories were well designed and regulated and that it was only the smaller and older units that were badly built and managed. In turn new problems emerged, especially that of enforcement, out of which developed considerations of the size, cost and effectiveness of government. To some degree these problems were made worse by the lack of expertly informed opinion; this is not surprising in view of the limited scientific understanding of the early nineteenth century. J. T. Ward, in *The Factory Movement* (q.v.), pointed out that in 1818 a Manchester Infirmary physician, Dr Edward Holme, could not be drawn to admit that 23 hours labour for children would necessarily be harmful, while Thomas Wilson, a Bingley surgeon, 'did not see that it was necessary' for children to have recreation. In the same enquiry Dr Edward Carbutt, also from Manchester Infirmary, explained that he and others were employed by a committee of cotton-masters.

Vested interests were deeply involved in the issues concerning factory reform, ranging from the factory owners who had sunk very substantial amounts of capital into textile production, to the spinners who sought to restrict their own hours of work, to maintain children's wages, to restrict the age of entry to employment and so forth. But gradually and in various ways, says J. T. Ward, 'groups of magistrates, medical practitioners and clergymen protested against children's long employment'. Enlightened factory owners swelled the chorus demanding reform. Thus opinion came to support Oastler's view – 'I maintain the Law *must* interfere'.

1 Child Labour and Adult Dependence

Duffers, scavengers and piecers

(a) Some of them were employed as duffers to collect the cotton as it came out of the carding machine; some as scavengers, whose duty it was to sweep the dust and flue (the fine particles of cotton) from under the machines; but the majority were piecers, who tied
5 together the threads that broke during the stretch, when the carriage with its revolving spindles moved away from the rollers.

> M. W. Thomas, *The Early Factory Legislation* (Bank Publishing Co, 1948), p 16

(b) Children are soon very dextrous at connecting broken ends with prepared cotton at the rollers, their small fingers being more active and endued with a quicker sensibility of feeling than those of grown
10 persons, and it is wonderful to see with what despatch they can raise a system, connect threads, and drop it again into work almost instantaneously.

> J. Aitkin, *A Description of the Country from thirty to forty miles around Manchester* (1795), quoted in M. W. Thomas, ibid

Questions

a What was a 'carding machine' (line 2)?
b Explain what was happening 'when the carriage with its revolving spindles moved away from the rollers' (lines 5–6).
c Comment on the child labour mentioned in extract b, bearing in mind the length of the working day.
★ d Explain contemporary attitudes to the employment of children.
★ e How did religious opinion view the moral value of child labour? How did John Wesley view idleness in children?

2 A Beneficial Division of Labour

(a) In proportion as machinery is improved in simplicity, and becomes more uniform in its action or motion, a lower class of labour is required for its management; and as women and children are thus enabled to produce those fabrics, which it formerly required
5 all the ingenuity, skill, and labour of the very best workmen to

furnish, the latter are set at liberty from the mere drudgery of manufacturing employment and are at leisure to engage in those more difficult and delicate operations, which the perpetual multiplication of machinery renders necessary.

> J. Kennedy, *Miscellaneous Papers* (1849), pp 43–4, quoted in M. W. Thomas, op cit

10 (b) The old and the young are essentially necessary to each other, and form a whole, and make a full and beneficial division of labour.

> V. Royle, *The Factory System Defended* (1833), p 23, quoted in M. W. Thomas, op cit

(c) In Glasgow spinning mills in the 1830's, one male spinner might work with a little piecer (or piecener), an outside piecer, and an inside piecer, ranging in age from 9 to 13 or 14 and over and
15 progressing in wages from about 2s. 6d. a week to about 6s. 3d. He engaged and paid them out of his own wages of £2, and usually employed his own children . . . . Children worked alongside adults throughout the working day which was normally twelve hours, but, in a rush of orders, might be far longer . . . . The group worked as a
20 team.

> U. R. Q. Henriques, *The Early Factory Acts and Their Enforcement* (Historical Association, 1971), p 2

Questions

a Explain what is meant by a 'lower class of labour' (lines 2–3).
b Explain the nature of the jobs that the women and children were expected to do. What were their future prospects?
★ c Was Kennedy's vision of the bright future for the skilled worker realistic? Consider the fortunes of the hand-loom weaver.
d Which children were first employed in textile mills and factories?
e What day-to-day problems do you consider might have emerged with which this group working 'as a team' had to cope (lines 19–20)?
f What do you think was the effect on a miner's earnings when he had to employ children other than his own? How was the older worker placed, when his children had left home?
g What would be the consequences for adult workers if the hours of children working in the mills were restricted?

3 The Campaign for Reform

(a) Medical opinion in Manchester

1. It appears that the children and others who work in the large cotton factories are peculiarly disposed to be affected by the

contagion of fever, and that when such infection is received, it is
rapidly propagated, not only amongst those who are crowded
5 together in the same apartments, but in the families and
neighbourhoods to which they belong.

2. The large factories are generally injurious to the constitution of
those employed in them, even where no particular diseases prevail,
from the close confinement which is enjoined, from the debilitating
10 effects of hot or impure air, and from want of the active exercises
which nature points out as essential to childhood and youth, to
invigorate the system, and to fit our species for the employments and
duties of manhood.

3. The untimely labour of the night, and the protracted labour of
15 the day, with respect to children, not only tends to diminish future
expectations as to the general sum of life and industry, by impairing
the strength and destroying the vital stamina of the rising
generation, but it too often gives encouragement to idleness,
extravagance and profligacy in the parents, who, contrary to the
20 order of nature, subsist in the oppression of their offspring.

4. It appears that the children employed in factories are generally
debarred from all opportunities of education, and from moral or
religious instruction.

5. From the excellent regulations which subsist in several cotton
25 factories, it appears that many of these evils may, in a considerable
degree, be obviated; we are therefore warranted by experience, and
are assured we shall have the support of the liberal proprietors of
these factories, in proposing an application for Parliamentary aid
. . . to establish a general system of laws for the wise, humane, and
30 equal government of all such works.

Report of the Board of Health at Manchester, 1796, quoted in
M. W. Thomas, op cit

Questions

a What, in the Board's view, were the causes of the rapid spread of
infection in the factories and their immediate neighbourhood?
b Why did the Board consider that factory work undermined the
well-being of the 'rising generation' (lines 17–18)?
c Why did the Board consider that the 'protracted labour of the
day' encouraged 'idleness, extravagance and profligacy' in the
parents (lines 14–19)? Was this a reasonable opinion to hold?
d What was the consequence of the lack of educational
opportunity?
e Were the proprietors of factories indeed 'liberal' and willing to
support 'laws for the wise, humane and equal government of all
such works' (lines 27–30)?

(b) The factory owners campaign against reform

Passed unanimously at a meeting in the Old Rock Tavern, Halifax, Mr James Ackroyd in the chair, March 5th, 1831.

1st. That this meeting views with alarm the measures proposed in the House of Commons, to curtail the hours of labour in mills or
5   factories, and to limit the ages of children employed in the same.

2nd. That the condition of those employed in worsted mills does not warrant the conclusion that the present usages of the trade are injurious to the health and comforts of this class of operatives; and that the present term of labour (viz. twelve hours per day) is not
10 attended with any consequences injurious to those employed, and is not more than adequate and necessary to provide for their livelihood.

3rd. That an enactment which will abridge the hours of labour, or limit the age of children employed in the worsted mills, will produce
15 the following effect:-

1st. It will cause a proportionate reduction of the wages of this class.

2nd. It will materially cripple the means of those who have large and young families, who, in many instances, are the main support
20 of their parents.

3rd. It will raise the price of goods to consumers, which will affect the home trade considerably, and will produce the most serious effects upon the prosperity of this district, by tending to foster the manufactures of foreign nations, our trade with whom
25 depends upon the advantageous terms on which we now supply them with goods . . . .

4th. It will throw out of employment and the means of existence numbers of children now beneficially engaged in worsted mills, and a corresponding proportion of wool-sorters, combers,
30 weavers, and all those other classes necessary to produce the present supply of goods.

5th. The agriculturalists will also feel the effects of the diminished consumption of wool in no small degree.

> Record of a meeting of the Master Worsted Spinners of Halifax, 1851, quoted in M. W. Thomas, op cit

Questions

a   Could the loss of child earnings 'materially cripple' large families (line 18)?

b   How valid were the economic arguments put forward by the Master Worsted Spinners of Halifax?

c   Why did the opponents of reform point out the effects upon agriculture?

d   Some manufacturers had already implemented and even exceeded the reforms that were introduced in 1833; who, then, were the manufacturers most likely to suffer as the result of the curtailment of child labour?

e What economic theories could the employers use to justify their resistance to factory reform?

(c) A reformer's opinions: Richard Oastler

(i) A Tory is one who, believing that the institutions of this country are calculated, as they were intended, to secure the prosperity and happiness of every class of society, wishes to maintain them in their original beauty, simplicity and integrity. He is tenacious of the rights
5 of all, but most of the poor and needy, because they require the shelter of the constitution and the laws more than other classes. A Tory is a staunch friend of Order, for the sake of Liberty; and knowing that our institutions are founded upon Christianity, he is of course a Christian, believing with S. Paul that each order of Society
10 is mutually dependent upon the others for peace and prosperity . . . I never changed my name, I never saw any charm in the word 'Conservative'. I am still an old-fashioned ultra-Tory.

> *The Fleet Papers*, I and 5 (30 January), 1841, quoted in M. W. Thomas (q.v.), op cit

(ii) I am not of the present school of 'Political Economists', 'Free Traders', 'Liberals', so-called 'Emigration Boards and Com-
15 mittees' I detest – I contend that the Labourer has the right to live on his Native Soil. . . . The Altar, the Throne and the Cottage should care alike in the protection of the Law.

Shall the Law refuse to protect the only property of the Poor, HIS LABOUR, because some few, unjust, unprincipled men refuse to
20 pay its value? I maintain the Law must interfere.

> *Leeds Intelligencer*, 12 December 1832, quoted in M. W. Thomas (q.v.), op cit

Questions

a Why did Oastler believe that the poor and needy most required the 'shelter of the constitution and the laws' (line 6)?

b What kind of attitude does Oastler show towards the working men and women?

★ c What were Emigration Boards and Committees?

d In what ways do Oastler's views differ from other reformers who sought the amelioration of the position of children in employment?

★ e Oastler is obviously looking backwards; of what kinds of legislation is he thinking?

★ f With which writer of the early nineteenth century can Oastler be compared?

* *g* Examine the contribution of the Ten Hour Movement, led by Oastler and others, to the achievement of factory reform.
* *h* Oastler clearly tried to distance himself from the Conservatives. Was he justified in thinking that Peel was unlikely to be sympathetic to his views?

(d) The factory commission's conclusions

From the whole of the evidence laid before us we find –

1st. That the children employed in all the principal branches of manufacture throughout the kingdom work during the same number of hours as the adults.

5   2nd. That the effects of labour during such hours are, in a great number of cases, permanent deterioration of the physical condition, the production of disease often wholly irremediable; and the partial or entire exclusion (by reason of excessive fatigue) from the means of obtaining adequate education and acquiring useful habits, or of

10 profiting by those means when afforded.

3rd. That at the age when children suffer these injuries from the labour they undergo, they are not free agents, but are let out to hire, the wages they earn being received and appropriated by their parents and guardians.

15 We are therefore of the opinion that a case is made out for the interference of the Legislature in behalf of the children employed in factories.

Parliamentary Papers, 1833, vol XX, pp 35–6

Questions

a What was the significance of setting up a Royal Commission to investigate the factories?

b What were 'useful habits' (line 9)?

c What were the permanent results of factory labour for children?

d What political economists were most likely to reject the 'interference of the Legislature' (line 16)?

e Explain the importance of the view that 'they are not free agents, but are let out to hire' (line 12).

* *f* Who took the leading part in producing the Commission's report? Of what importance was that contribution?

IV   Factory Reform: Legislation

Introduction

While the real course of events and the conflicts of opinion and philosophy was much more complex than this chapter suggests, it is possible to see in factory reform legislation the development outlined in the General Introduction, a development repeated in the enactments concerned with coal mines. Reform acts of greater and wider force and compass were shaped in response to the knowledge brought to parliament by knowledgeable men, to the evidence collected by enquiry and commission and, in time, to the recommendations of inspectors working at first hand with the problems of enforcement and supervision. The factory acts showed, where needed, greater awareness of technical problems and greater draughting efficiency; they culminated in a consolidating statute in 1878. Thereafter the tone of the legislation assumes a much more positive character; the permissive nature of earlier legislation has been superceded by a more determined expression of central will.

The first act to attempt state regulation of the lives of the labouring classes and their workplaces was passed in 1802. Inspiration for the act came from Sir Robert Peel the elder, a highly successful factory owner, who owed much of his good fortune to the employment of child labour. His act dealt with the well-being of the apprentices who, while unwanted in the London workhouses, constituted a valued source of labour in the water-powered and remote northern mills. Peel's second initiative, which reached the statute book in 1819, was severely curbed by the energetic actions of factory owners now thoroughly alert to the dangers that might come from further legislation. Both laws were broadly conceived; taken together, they covered the ages and hours of workers, the conditions in which they worked, the special needs of apprentices, as well as elementary education and moral direction for the young. Sir Cam Hobhouse continued Peel's activity; further legislation came in 1825 and 1831. All four of these enactments, however, suffered from one irreparable weakness: there was no effective means of enforcement built into them. This deficiency was remedied by the act of 1833; from this beginning developed the Factory Inspectorate. The act, based upon solid evidence, set up central direction and uniformity of administration as Benthamite principles urged; it dealt with the huge numbers of children and young people drawn into factory work. Most employers saw the need for an educated workforce and so in 1833 the attempt was made to force some education upon the young. When, however, Sir James Graham in 1843 tried to strengthen the educational provisions for young people, an intense argument broke out among the various churches in Britain. His proposals were held greatly to benefit the Church of England; the dissenting churchmen and congregations bombarded parliament with petitions to seek the destruction of what they thought was discriminating legislation. J. T. Ward, the historian of the Factory Movement, thought the result highly significant: 'The failure of the 1843 bill did not long postpone factory reform. But the establishment of a national educational system, towards which Graham was reaching, was held back for nearly thirty years'.

Restriction of the hours of children and young people faced factory owners with the problem of integrating the reduced working day of the young with the hours of adult workers. One of the consequences was a type of shift work known as the relay system. Meanwhile the working men had been campaigning for short-time working, particularly the ten-hour day. The Ten Hour Movement, led by Richard Castler, apparently achieved its goal in 1847, only to find its hopes dashed by the law courts. Yet by 1853 the working week of all factory employers was quite altered by the gathering pace of change over the previous 50 years.

The model of industrial control, forged for the textile mills and factories, was gradually followed in more and more industries. Yet even as these problems of industrial regulation were being overcome, new troubles emerged. Charles Booth in particular helped to bring public attention to the horrors of the 'sweated trades'; his *Life and Labour of the People in London* revealed the conditions of the East End and especially of the immigrant Jewish population. Remedial legislation was passed towards the end of the century. Some workers, such as those employed in the retail trades, remained very vulnerable to long hours of work and low rates of pay, but their conditions also came under parliamentary scrutiny at the same period of time.

1 The Health and Morals of Apprentices Act, 1802

Whereas it hath of late become a Practice in Cotton and Woollen mills, and in Cotton and Woollen factories, to employ a great number of Male and Female Apprentices, and other Persons in the same building; in consequence of which certain Regulations are
5 become necessary to preserve the Health and Morals of such Apprentices and other Persons; be it therefore enacted . . .

ii . . . That all and every the Rooms and Apartments in or belonging to any such Mill or Factory shall, Twice at least in every year, be well and sufficiently washed in Quick Lime and Water over
10 every Part the Walls and Cieling (sic) thereof; and that due Care and Attention shall be paid . . . to provide a sufficient Number of Windows and Openings . . . to insure a proper Supply of fresh Air.

iii . . . That every such Master or Mistress shall constantly supply every Apprentice, during the term of his or her Apprenticeship, with
15 two whole and complete sets of cloathing, with suitable Linen, Stockings, Hats and Shoes.

iv . . . That no Apprentice . . . shall be employed or compelled to work for more than Twelve Hours in any One Day . . . no Apprentice shall be employed or compelled to work upon any
20 Occasion whatever, between the Hours of Nine of the Clock at Night and Six of the Clock in the Morning.

vi . . . That every such Apprentice shall be instructed, in some part of every working Day . . . in Reading, Writing and Arithmetick, or either of them according to the Age and Abilities of
25 such Apprentice, by some discreet and proper Person.

vii . . . That the Room or Apartment in which any Male Apprentices shall sleep, shall be entirely separate and distinct from the Room or Apartment in which any Female Apprentice shall sleep and that no more than Two Apprentices shall in any Case sleep in the
30 same bed.

viii . . . That every Apprentice . . . shall, for the Space of One Hour at least every Sunday, be instructed and examined in the Principles of the Christian Religon.

ix . . . That the Justices of the Peace . . . shall . . . appoint Two
35 Persons, not interested in, or in any such Way connected with, any such Mills or Factories . . . (who) shall have full Power and Authority from Time to Time throughout the Year, to enter into and inspect any such Mill or Factory.
42 Geo III, c. 73

Questions

a   How far did the Act of 1802 go to meet the requirements of the Board of Health of Manchester?

b   Who were the apprentices who worked in the textile mills and factories? Where did they come from? In which factories was their labour particularly needed?

★ c   Who brought this measure before parliament?

d   What were the principles that the Act identified?

e   Why was the responsibility for implementing the Act left to the Justices of the Peace?

f   How did the Act provide for the moral education of apprentices?

2 The Factory Act of 1819

(a) . . . no child shall be employed in any Description of Work, for the spinning of Cotton or Wool into Yarn, or in any previous Preparation of such Wool, until he or she shall have attained the full Age of Nine Years.

5   ii . . . no Person, being under the Age of Sixteen Years, shall be employed in any Description of work whatsoever, in spinning Cotton Wool into Yarn . . . for more than Twelve Hours in any One Day, exclusive of the necessary time for meals; such Twelve Hours to be between the Hours of Five o'Clock in the Morning and Nine

10   o'Clock in the Evening.

    iii . . . there shall be allowed to every such Person, in the course of every Day, not less than Half an Hour to Breakfast, and not less than One full Hour for Dinner.

        59 Geo III c. 66

(b) It was because the Act of 1819 opened the way to further and
15   more far-reaching reforms that it occupies so important a place in the development of factory legislation . . . it broke down barriers. The State had intervened between employers and employed, and on the narrow foundation of this fundamental principle the dreaming of the reformers and innovators was to rear a mighty fabric.

        M. W. Thomas, op cit, p 27

Questions

a   List carefully the restrictions upon the use of the labour of children and young persons by 1819.

b   How long did the makers of the Act envisage a young person would spend in a factory in one day?

c   How did the Act of 1819 in matters of principle differ from the enactment of 1802?

d   Why could M. W. Thomas say the later statute 'broke down barriers' (line 16)?

e   What is meant by a 'mighty fabric' (line 19)?

3   Rules, Regulations and Orders

. . . no Person under Eighteen Years of Age should be allowed to work in the Night, (that is to say), between the Hours of Half past Eight o'Clock in the Evening and Half past Five o'Clock in the Morning in or about any Cotton, Worsted, Hemp, Flax, Tow,
5   Linen, or Silk Mill or Factory wherein Steam or Water or any other mechanical Power is or shall be used.

    ii. no Person under the age of Eighteen Years shall be employed . . . more than Twelve Hours in any One Day, nor more than Sixty-nine Hours in any One Week.

10   vii. it shall not be lawful for any Person whatsoever to employ in any Factory or Mill, except in Mills for the Manufacture of Silk, any Child who shall not have completed his of her Ninth Year of Age.

    viii. it shall not be lawful . . . to employ, keep, or to allow to
15 remain in any Factory or Mill for a longer time than Forty-eight Hours in any One Week, nor for a longer time than Nine Hours in any One Day any Child who shall not have completed his or her Eleventh Year of Age (this age was successively raised to 12 and then to 13).

20   ix. all Children and young Persons whose Hours of work are regulated . . . shall be entitled to the following Holidays, videlicet, on Christmas and Good Friday the entire Day, and not fewer than Eight Half Days besides in every Year.

    xi. it shall not be lawful for any Person to employ . . . any Child
25 who shall not have completed his or her Eleventh Year of Age without such Certificate as is herein-after mentioned.

    xii. for the Purpose of obtaining the Certificate herein-before required . . . the Child shall personally appear before some Surgeon or Physician . . . and unless the Surgeon or Physician . . . shall
30 certify his having had a personal Examination of such Child, and also that such Child is of the ordinary Strength and Appearance of Children of or exceeding the Age of Nine Years . . . such Child shall not be employed in any Factory or Mill.

    xvii. whereas it appears that . . . the Laws for the Regulation of
35 the Labour of Children in Factories have been evaded . . . it shall be lawful . . . to appoint . . . Four Persons to be Inspectors of Factories and Places where the Labour of Children and young Persons under eighteen Years is employed.

    xviii. the said Inspectors . . . shall have Power and are hereby
40 required to make all such Rules, Regulations and Orders as may be necessary for the due Execution of this Act.

    xx. every Child herein-before restricted to the Performance of Forty-eight Hours of Labour in any one Week shall . . . attend some School to be chosen by the Parents or Guardian of such Child, or
45 such School as may be appointed by any Inspector.

    xxi. it shall not be lawful to employ . . . any Child restricted by this Act to the Performance of Forty-eight Hours of Labour in any One Week, unless such Child shall, on Monday in every Week next after the Commencement of such Employment . . . give to the
50 Factory Master . . . a Schoolmaster's Ticket or Voucher, certifying that such Child has for Two Hours at least for Six out of Seven Days of the Week next preceding attended his School, excepting in the Cases of Sickness.

    xxii. wherever it shall appear to any Inspector that a new or
55 additional School is necessary or desirable to enable the Children employed in any Factory to obtain the Education required by this

Act, such Inspector is hereby authorised to establish and procure the Establishment of such School.

An Act to regulate the Labour of Children and Young Persons, 1833

Questions

a What limitations were placed upon the working hours of children and young persons? How far do they mark a development upon earlier legislation?

★ b How was it possible to establish the age of a child? When was it made compulsory to register births and deaths?

★ c How reliable was the opinion of medical men likely to be? When was the General Medical Council set up?

d Why was the maximum number of working hours per week laid down as well as the maximum for any single day?

★ e Why did clauses xx and xxi prove so difficult to enforce?

f Why did clause xxii, which stands on its own, remain inoperative?

g Explain the significance of clauses xvii and xviii.

h The Inspectors were given the power to make 'all such Rules, Regulations and Order as may be necessary' (lines 40–41). What kinds of rules and regulations were needed?

i In some industries a different education qualification was required – the ability to read. Do you think the Factory Act of 1833 was wise in simply demanding a certificate of school attendance?

4 Plans for Relays

Where the work begins at 6, and breakfast is from 8 to 8½, dinner from 12½ to 1½, tea from 5½ to 6, and the mill stops at 8 o'clock.

Suppose three sets of children of thirty each, called A, B and C.

A.	Work from 6 to 8 . . .	2 hours
	8½ to 10½ . . .	2 hours
	1½ to 5½ . . .	<u>4</u> hours
		8

Go to school from 10½ to 12½, and have the evening for recreation.

B.	Work from 10½ to 12½ . . .	2 hours
	1½ to 5½ . . .	4 hours
	6 to 8 . . .	<u>2</u> hours
		8

Go to school from 8½ to 10½, and have the morning before breakfast for recreation.

C.	Work from 6 to 8 . . .	2 hours
	8½ to 12½ . . .	4 hours
	6 to 8 . . .	2 hours
		8

And go to school from 1½ to 3½, and have the afternoon for recreation.

All the changes take place at meal-hours except one, viz, between breakfast and dinner, when half of the number at work go out, to be replaced by others.

Parliamentary Papers, 1837, vol XXXI, p 68

Questions

a The use of relays or shifts was devised to make it possible to continue to use child labour in textile factories; the scheme given above was devised by the Factory Inspector, Leonard Horner. Does this system look workable?

b What operating problems would the relay system pose for adult and juvenile workers?

c What administrative problems did the factory face in using relays, if the Inspectors were to be satisfied that the law was being observed?

d If the factory owner did not use relays in his factory, how otherwise could he deal with the children employed in his works?

5 Broader Considerations

xix . . . no Child or young Person shall be employed in any Part of a Factory in which the wet-spinning of Flax, Hemp, Jute, or Tow is carried on, unless sufficient Means shall be employed and continued for protecting the Workers from being wetted.

xx . . . no Child or any young Person shall be allowed to clean any Part of the mill-gearing in a Factory while the same is in motion.

xxi . . . every Fly-wheel directly connected with the Steam Engine or Water-wheel or other mechanical Power, whether in the Engine House or not, and every Part of a Steam Engine and Water-wheel and every Hoist or Teagle, near to which Children or young Persons are liable to pass or be employed, and all Parts of the mill-gearing in a Factory, shall be securely fenced; and every Wheel-race not otherwise secured shall be fenced close to the Edge of the Wheel-race.

xxiv . . . One of her Majesty's Principal Secretaries of State, on the Report and Recommendation of an Inspector, may empower

such Inspector to direct One or more Actions to be brought in the
Name and on behalf of any Person who shall be reported by such
Inspector to have received any bodily injury from the machinery of
20 any factory.
    xxxi . . . it shall be lawful to employ any Child Ten Hours in any
One Day on Three alternate Days of every Week . . . Provided
always that the Parent or Person having direct benefit from the
Wages of any Child so employed shall cause such Child to attend
25 some school for at least five Hours . . . on each Week Day preceding
such Day of Employment in the Factory.
    xxxii . . . no Female above the Age of eighteen Years shall be
employed in any Factory save for the same time and in the same
Manner as young Persons may be employed in Factories.
    Factory Act, 1844

Questions

a What is the significance of clause xxiv?
b What new principles were introduced by the other clauses of the
     Factory Act of 1844?
c Clause xxxi made the 'half-time' system possible; did it mark an
     advance upon the use of relays?

6 The Ten Hour Day: Granted and Denied

(a) ii . . . no Person under the age of eighteen Years shall be
employed in any such Mill or Factory . . . for more than Ten Hours
in any One Day, nor for more than Fifty-eight Hours in any One
Week.
5   iii . . . the Restrictions respectively by this Act imposed as regards
the working of Persons under the age of Eighteen Years shall extend
to Females above the Age of Eighteen Years.
    Factory Act, 1847

(b) Ryder v. Mills
    This question depends entirely on the proper construction to be
put on those Acts, and more particularly on the 7th Victoria, cap. 15
10 (1844). These Acts must be construed according to the established
rules for the construction of statutes. In courts of law we have only to
ascertain the meaning of the words used by the Legislature, and
when that is ascertained we have to carry it into effect, and we are not
to enquire whether the enactments are dictated by sound policy or
15 not; that question is exclusively for the consideration of Parliament
. . . Is, then, the owner of a factory liable to the penalty in respect to
the employment of a child or young person in the manner stated?
    The Act imposes a penalty, and therefore according to the
established rule, must be construed strictly; that is, a man is not to be

20 restrained from the liberty which he has by acting as he pleases, and rendered liable to a punishment, unless the law has plainly said that he shall. It is not enough that we conjecture, even strongly, that it was the intention of the Legislature to have prohibited the act. There must be words indicating plainly and clearly that it has done so, and,
25 applying this rule of construction, we do not think that there are words in the statutes sufficiently plain and clear to render the conduct of the defendant in the case above-mentioned liable to punishment.

Mr Baron Parke explains the judgement of the Court of Exchequer, 8 February 1850, in the test case of Ryder v. Mills, quoted in C. C. Driver, *Tory Radical, Life of Richard Oastler* (New York, O.U.P., 1946)

Questions

a What changes were introduced by the 1847 Act?
b What was likely to be the effect of the Act upon the overall manning of factories?
★ c What is a 'test case'?
d What was the judgement given by the Court of Exchequer upon the Act of 1847?

7 Ten Hours – the Normal Day

(a) no young Person and no Female above the age of Eighteen Years shall be employed in any Factory before Six of the clock in the Morning or after Six of the Clock in the evening of any Day.

An Act to amend the Acts relating to Labour in Factories (1850)

no Child shall be employed in any Factory before Six of the Clock in
5 the Morning or after Six of the Clock in the Evening of any Day.

An Act further to regulate the Employment of Children in Factories (1853)

Questions

a What was the maximum number of hours children, young persons and women could be kept in a factory after 1853?
b How many hours were allocated to meal times?
c What was the effect of these Acts upon the relay system?
d How had the working day of male adult factory workers changed since 1819?

8 The Sweating System

In conformity with your directions I have made enquiries into what is known as the 'sweating system' at the East End of London, especially in the tailoring trade, and I have now to submit the following report.

5   The system may be defined as one under which sub-contractors undertake to do work in their own houses or small workshops, and employ others to do it, making a profit for themselves by the difference between the contract prices and the wages they pay their assistants. The scale of business of such contractors varies greatly,

10   many who are called sweaters employing one or two assistants only, while workshops in which ten, twenty or even thirty to forty are employed are also numerous . . . .

The demand for cheap clothes, irrespective of quality, has continually tended to bring down the rates of remuneration of the

15   least skilled of the workers, and has caused the introduction of the most minute systems of subdivided labour. The cheaper branches of the trade have been completely cut up into sections . . . . We have cutters, basters, machinists, pressers, fellers, buttonhole workers and general workers, all brought to bear upon the construction of a

20   coat. The learning of any one of these branches is, naturally, so much easier than the acquisition of the whole trade that immense numbers of people of both sexes and all ages have rushed into the cheap tailoring trade as the readiest means of finding employment . . . .

The character of the workshops, or places used as workshops,

25   varies considerably. The smaller sweaters, as has been already remarked, use part of their dwelling accommodation, and in the vast majority of cases work is carried on under conditions in the highest degree filthy and insanitary. In small rooms not more than nine or ten feet square, heated by a coke fire for the pressers' irons, and at

30   night lit by flaring gas jets, six, eight, ten, and even a dozen workers may be crowded. The conditions of the Public Health Acts, and of the Factory and Workshops Regulations Acts, are utterly disregarded, and existing systems of inspection are entirely inadequate to enforce their provisions . . . .

35   Where work is carried on under such a system and such conditions little is to be expected from the people employed, who may be said to exist but cannot by any possibility enjoy life.

Parliamentary Papers, 1888, vol XX, App G, quoted in W. D. Handcock, *EHD*, vol XII(2) (Unwin, 1952)

Questions

a   How did the 'sweating system' operate?
b   Why were people drawn to work in such conditions?
c   Why was there such a demand for cheap clothes (line 13)?
d   Why were sweat shops able to continue to exist in the face of all the legislation that had been laid down?

9 Special Rules and Requirements

(a) 8(i) Where the Secretary of State certifies that in his opinion any machinery of process or particular description of manual labour used in a factory or workshop . . . is injurious or dangerous to health or dangerous to life and limb, either generally or in the case of women,
5 children, or any other class of person, or that the provision of fresh air is insufficient, or that the quantity of dust generated or inhaled in any factory or workshop is dangerous or injurious to health, the chief inspector may serve on the occupier of the factory or workshop a notice in writing either proposing special rules or requiring the
10 adoption of such special measures as to appear to the chief inspector to be reasonably practicable and to meet the necessities of the case.

27(i) The occupier of every factory or workshop . . . shall . . . keep in the prescribed form and with the prescribed particulars lists showing the names of all persons directly employed by him.

Factories Act, 1891

15 (b) The regulation of wages

2(i) The Board of Trade shall, if practicable, establish one or more Trade Boards constituted in accordance with regulations made under this Act for any trade to which this Act applies or any branch of work in the trade.
20 4(i) Trade Boards shall . . . fix minimum rates of wages for timework in their trades . . . and may also fix general minimum rates for piece-work for their trades.

11(i) The Board of Trade may make regulations with respect to the constitution of Trade Boards which shall consist of members
25 representing employers and members representing workers . . . in equal proportions and of the appointed members.

Trade Boards Act, 1909

Questions

a By what standard could work premises be judged after 1891?
b How is this standard different from the requirements of earlier factory acts?
c What is the purpose of clause 27(i) of the 1891 Act?
d How could the Trade Boards Act help to prevent the exploitation of sweated labour?

10 Shops Act, 1912

1. (1) On at least one week day in each week a shop assistant shall not be employed about the business of a shop after half-past one o'clock in the afternoon.

2. (1) No person under the age of eighteen years shall be
5 employed in or about a shop for a longer period than seventy-four hours, including meal times in any one week.

3. (1) In all rooms of a shop where female shop-assistants are employed in the serving of customers, the occupier of the shop shall provide seats behind the counter . . . in the proportion of not less than one seat to every three female shop-assistants employed in each room.

Questions

a How long could a young person be expected to work in a shop in one day if regular opening hours were kept?

b Why was it so much more difficult for shop workers to achieve the improvements in working life enjoyed by factory workers?

V The National Conscience Aroused: Reform in the Mines

Introduction

Althopp's Factory Act of 1833 was the outcome of extensive investigation into working conditions, enquiries which fitted into the growing pattern of research, measurement and assessment characteristic of the period. However, inspectors in factories and schools discovered that conditions in mines were worse than those in the factories. Mining disasters, such as those at Felling Colliery and St Hilda's pit in 1839, together with the Report of the Select Committee on Accidents in Mines (1835) and the investigations of the South Shields Committee brought the problems of mine safety and working conditions increasingly to public notice, even outside mining areas. By contrast the question of mine reform was catapulted into the front rank of topics needing urgent public consideration and treatment by the Report of the Commissioners on the Labour of Women and Children in Mines (1842). The Report, and in particular the drawings it contained, brought the problem vividly before the whole nation.

To produce reform by statute was regarded by many experienced in the ways of the mining industry as being a very difficult task. It was thought that legislation would be able only to deal with general rules to govern mining practices and that those general rules would be very difficult to formulate. The miners lived and worked in communities that were remote (especially before the growth of the railway network) and strongly identified. Within these communities a vigorous, especially oral, tradition developed. Not only were the communities easily identifiable socially but they also faced unique working conditions; the nature of the local coal seams and geological conditions affected the character of mine workings, the rate of extraction and, therefore, the labour involved, the earnings of the miners themselves, as well as the profitability of the mine workings.

The experience of the passage of Ashley's bill in 1842 through parliament was hardly unique; opposition whittled it down considerably, the House of Lords being especially hostile. Yet opposition to the proposals, which prohibited women from the mines and regulated the work of boys, developed in some mining areas. The large number of women, the very people the Act was designed to protect, now put out of work, suffered serious loss of earnings; they had no other skills, experience or opportunities for work to fall back upon.

It took a long time to produce a general code of safety for the mines; the temporary measures passed in 1850 and 1855 helped to give valuable experience and the government felt justified in 1860 in producing permanent legislation. Much had been learned over the previous two decades. General rules were developed and extended and the need for special rules, specific to particular mines, recognised. The Consolidating Act of 1872 ensured competent management and the expansion of the powers of the inspectorate. The Mines Act of 1887 marked further, and essential, progress; it dealt with particular, but important problems: coal–dust explosions, shot firing and ambulance work. On a pattern similar to these developments in coal-mining, legislation was introduced making provision relating to mines other than coal mines (Mines Regulation Act, 1872) and laying down regulations for all types of mining, quarrying, factories and workshops (Notice of Accidents Act, 1906).

One aspect of the 1860 Act, which unwittingly had important repercussions for industrial relations, was the introduction of the checkweighman into British coalmines. The purpose of this innovation was to remedy miners' grievances over the calculation of amounts of coal recovered and the associated pay. While achieving this objective, the new office also produced leaders for the miners, leaders who could not easily be browbeaten and who frequently combined union posts with their mine duties. The mine unions were greatly strengthened by this development in the years of greater militancy at the turn of the century. That greater aggressiveness and changing political attitudes helped to produce the Coal Mines Regulation Act (1908) and the Coal Mines (Minimum Wage) Act (1912).

1 Why Factory Reform Came First

In recommending legislative restriction of the labour of children, as not being free agents, and not being able to protect themselves, we have been careful not to lose sight of the practical limits within which alone any general rule admits of application. We have not found
5 these limits in the greater or lesser intensity, or in the greater or lesser unwholesomeness of infant labour in factories. It appears in evidence, that of all employments to which children are subjected, those carried on in factories are amongst the least laborious, and of all departments of indoor labour, amongst the least unwholesome. It is
10 in evidence, that boys employed in collieries are subjected at a very early age to very severe labour, that cases of deformity are more

common and accidents more frequent amongst them than amongst children employed in factories . . . .

We are induced . . . briefly to state the grounds which appear to
15 justify that interference with factories, as distinguished from collieries, or from establishments of a domestic nature. Children employed in factories, as a distinct class, form a very considerable proportion of the infant population. We have found that the numbers are rapidly increasing, not only in proportion to the
20 increase of the population employed in manufacturing industry, but in consequence of the tendency of improvements of machinery to throw more and more of the work upon children, to the displacement of adult labour. The children are assembled together in large numbers . . . . Their daily entrance into and dismissal from
25 the factories takes place with the regularity of military discipline.

First Report of the Commission of Enquiry into Factories, *Parliamentary Papers*, 1833, vol XX, pp 35–6, 55–6, quoted in Evans (ed.), *Social Policy, 1830–1914* (Routledge and Kegan Paul, 1978)

Questions

a Did the Commissioners find work in collieries more dangerous and arduous than that in factories?

b Why were more and more children being employed in factories?

c What particular aspects of child labour in factories caused concern?

d Why was there an apparently greater concern 'to justify that interference with factories, as distinguished from collieries' (lines 14–16)?

★ e Why was mine reform so long in coming?

2 'Practices Peculiar to a Few Districts'

12. That, in the East of Scotland, a much larger proportion of Children and Young Persons are employed in these mines than in other districts, many of whom are girls: and that the chief part of their labour consists in carrying the coals on their backs up steep
5 ladders.

23. That there are moreover two practices peculiar to a few districts which deserve the highest reprobation, namely, first, the practice not unknown in some of the smaller mines in Yorkshire, and common in Lancashire, of employing ropes that are unsafe for
10 letting down and drawing up the workpeople: and second, the practice, occasionally met with in Yorkshire, and common in Derbyshire and Lancashire, of employing boys at the steam-engines for letting down and drawing up the workpeople.

24. That in general the Children and Young Persons who work in
15 these mines have sufficient food, and, when above ground, decent
and comfortable clothing, their usually high rate of wages securing
to them these advantages; but in many cases more especially in some
parts of Yorkshire, in Derbyshire, in South Gloucestershire, and
very generally in the East of Scotland, the food is poor in quality and
20 insufficient in quantity; the Children themselves say that they have
not enough to eat; and the sub-commissioners describe them as
covered with rags, and state that the common excuse they make for
confining themselves to their homes on the Sundays, instead of
taking recreation in the fresh air, or attending a place of worship, is
25 that they have no clothes to go in . . . in general, however, the
Children who are in this unhappy case are the Children of idle and
dissolute parents, who spend the hard-earned wages of their
offspring at the public house.

> Report of the Commission of the Labour of Women and
> Children in Mines (1842), quoted in G. I I. Young and W. D.
> Handcock, *EHD*, vol XII (I)

Questions

a What was the principal employment of child and female labour in
   Scottish mines?
b What particularly dangerous practices did the Commissioners
   identify? What was so dangerous in using boys to run the
   winding gear?
c What was the general standard of living in most mining
   communities?
d Can you think of any causes (inherent in mining) for child neglect
   other than 'idle and dissolute' attitudes?

3   Thin Seams and Thick

(a) High Green George Chambers; Employ undertakers who
contract for getting coal from very thin seams. Horses used and there
is fire damp.

Barnsley Daay and Ottibell; 198 feet deep shaft 1 foot six inch wide
5 ropes used and wooden conductors; 1 Ten foot thick seam; winding
wheels large and 2 corves drawn at once; large gates; no females; fire
damp.

> J. Goodchild, ms., Cusworth Hall, Doncaster, quoted by
> Addy and Power, *The Industrial Revolution* (Longman, 1976),
> p 105

(b) Hunshelf Bank Webster and Peannes; a very small day pit, the
thin seam with gates 24″ to 30″; there are no horses and boys and girls
10 hurry together using belts and chains for hauling tubs.

Elsecar Earl Fitzwilliam; 80 foot shaft using round ropes and iron conductors for winding; seam 6 feet thick. It is an extensive colliery with large wide gates; Few children employed and all males; Horses are used and there is fire damp.
> Ibid

Questions

a How thick were the coal seams in each of these mines?
b What is 'fire damp' (line 3)?
c Why and where were horses used (line 2)?
d Where were children most likely to be employed? Why was this so?
e How could the thickness of the coal seams, then, be linked indirectly to the character of the mining communities?

4 The Character of Mining Communities

The parishes to which the inquiry refers are situated in the north-eastern angle of the mountain range which extends across a large part of South Wales. They comprise a tract of country about 20 miles east and west, and 10 miles north and south, forming an
5   irregular triangle . . . . From the northern boundary-line of this district, or the base of the triangle, six parallel valleys run off in the direction of north and south. Towards the heads of these valleys most of the largest iron-works, with the population clustered around them, may be marked on the map by dark spots . . . . The
10   people are for the most part collected together in masses of from 4,000 to 10,000. Their houses are ranged round the works in rows, sometimes two to five deep, sometimes three storeys high. They rarely contain less than from one to six lodgers in addition to the members of the family, and afford most scanty accommodation for
15   so many inmates. It is not unusual to find that 10 individuals of various age and sex occupy three beds in two small rooms.
    The entire population of these five parishes, according to the lowest estimate given by persons most conversant with each, amounts to 85,000. It is perceived by them that their children are sure
20   of being able to gain an ample livelihood at an early age, without the aid of 'learning'. The parents are, therefore, apt to believe that their superiors are actuated by some selfish motive in endeavouring to induce them to send their children to school . . . . (The boys) leave their homes at an early age, if they find that they can be boarded
25   cheaper elsewhere, and they spend the surplus of their wages in smoking, drinking and gambling. Boys of 13 will not infrequently boast that they have taken to smoking before they were 12. All

parental control is soon lost. Shortly after the age of 16 they begin to earn men's wages. Early marriages are very frequent.

Seymour Tremenheere, Inspector of Schools, *Parliamentary Papers*, 1840, vol XI, pp 208–13, quoted in G. M. Young and W. D. Handcock, op cit

Questions

★ *a* Identify the Merthyr Tydfil area on a map.

b Do you agree that these mining communities were remote, isolated and inward-looking?

c Why were the houses 'ranged round the works in rows, sometimes two to five deep' (lines 11–12)?

d Explain the view of the local population towards compulsory education. Was that judgement fair?

e Why did boys leave home 'at an early age' (line 24)?

f Was work easily available and well paid?

g Can you think of reasons why the miners' accommodation was 'scanty' (line 14)?

5 Child and Female Labour

258. Report of the Commission on the labour of women and children in mines (1842)

Parlty. Papers, 1842/XIII.

(a) First Report. Tables of Proportion of Children and Young People employed in different Districts

Proportion (nearly) of Females to adult Males, and of Females under age to Males under age.

Districts	Adults	From 13 to 18	Under 13
Yorkshire	1 to 45	1 to 28	1 to 25
Lancashire	1 to 12	1 to 13	1 to 37
EAST OF SCOTLAND			
Mid Lothian	1 to 3	1 to 5½	1 to 20
East Lothian	1 to 3	1 to 3½	1 to 10
West Lothian	1 to 5	1 to 7	1 to 10
Stirlingshire	1 to 4½	1 to 8	1 to 10
Clackmannanshire	1 to 5	1 to 5	1 to 11½
Fifeshire	1 to 5½	1 to 10	1 to 30
WALES			
Glamorganshire	1 to 53	1 to 53	1 to 83
Pembrokeshire	1 to 2½	1 to 8½	1 to 53

Quoted in G. M. Young and W. D. Handcock, op cit, vol XII(1), pp 972–3

Table No. I.—England

Districts	Adults		13 to 18		Under 13		Total of children and young persons to 1000 adult males	Proportion of children and young persons in the whole number employed	Proportion of children in the whole number under 18
	Males	Fem.	Males	Fem.	Males	Fem.			
Leicestershire	1000	—	227	—	180	—	407	Two-sevenths.	Much more than one-third.
Derbyshire	1000	—	240	—	167	—	407	Two-sevenths.	Much more than one-third.
Yorkshire	1000	22	352	36	246	41	675	Upwards of one-third.	Much more than one-third.
Lancashire	1000	86	352	79	195	27	653	Upwards of one-third.	Upwards of one-third.
South Durham	1000	—	226	—	184	—	410	Two-sevenths.	Much more than one-third.
Northumberland and North Durham	1000	—	266	—	186	—	452	Nearly one-third.	Much more than one-third.

Table No. IV.—Wales

Districts	Adults		13 to 18		Under 13		Total of children and young persons to 1000 adult males	Proportion of children and young persons in the whole number employed	Proportion of children in the whole number under 18
	Males	Fem.	Males	Fem.	Males	Fem.			
Monmouthshire	1000	—	302	—	154	—	456	Nearly one-third.	One-third.
Glamorganshire	1000	19	239	19	157	12	427	Approaching one-third.	Much more than one-third.
Pembrokeshire	1000	424	366	119	196	19	700	One-third.	More than one-third.

Questions

a Where was the labour of children and teenagers most and least used?
b Where was female adult labour most and least employed?
c Where was female child and teenage labour most needed?

6 The Collier Lass

My name's Polly Parker, I come o'er from Worsley.
My father and mother work in the coal mine.
Our family's large, we have got seven children,
So I am obliged to work in the same mine.
5   And as this is my fortune, I know you feel sorry
That in such employment my days I shall pass,
But I keep up my spirits, I sing and look merry
Although I am but a poor collier lass.

By the greatest of dangers each day I'm surrounded.
10   I hang in the hair by a rope or a chain.
The mine may fall in, I may be killed or wounded,
May perish by damp or the fire of the train.
And what would you do if it were not for our labour?
In wretched starvation your days you would pass,
15   While we could provide you with life's greatest blessing.
Then do not despise the poor collier lass.

All the day long you may say we are buried,
Deprived of the light and the warmth of the sun.
And often at nights from our bed we are hurried;
20   The water is in and barefoot we run.
And though we go ragged and black are our faces,
As kind and as free as the best we'll be found,
And our hearts are as white as your lords in fine places,
Although we're poor colliers that work underground.

From 'The Collier Lass' in A. L. Lloyd, *Folk Song in England*
(Panther Arts, 1969)

Questions

a Explain the meaning of hanging 'by a rope or a chain' (line 10).
★ b What is the meaning of 'damp or the fire of the train' (line 12)?
c What is life's 'greatest blessing' (line 15)?
d What event has compelled the miners to rush to the mine (line 19)?
e How does Polly Parker react to life in the mine?
f Does she think she will ever be able to leave such employment?
★ g How important is folk song as a source of historical evidence?

7 The Miner's Bond

Memorandum of Agreement, made the sixteenth day of March in
the year of our Lord 1833 between the owners of Seghill Colliery, of
the one part and several other persons whose names or marks are
hereunto subscribed of the other part.
5   The said owners to hereby retain and hire, the said several other
parties hereto from the fifth day of April next ensuing, until the fifth
day of April which will be in the year 1834, to hew, work, fill, drive
and put coals and do such other work as may be necessary for
carrying on the said colliery, as they shall be required or directed to
10   do by the said owners . . . at the respective rates and prices, and on
the terms, conditions, and stipulations, and subject to and under the
penalties and forfeitures, hereinafter specified and declared; that is to
say, FIRST – The said owners agree to pay the said parties hereby
hired, once a fortnight, upon the usual and accustomed day, the
15   wages by them earned, at the following rates, namely to each hewer
for every score of coals wrought out of the whole mine, each score to
consist of twenty corves and each corf to contain coals sufficient to
fill solidly the standard Coal Tub used at the said colliery – or by
weight coals sufficient to weigh 6 cwt in the High Main Seam where
20   the seam if 3ft 10ins in height and upwards 6s 10d per score, and
where the seam if 3ft 6ins and under 7s 1d score of Round coals
handpicked – Should any Hewer be found breaking his coals
unnecessarily in either seam to be fined 2s 6d for every offence. –
Each person for whom the said Owner shall provide a Dwelling
25   House as part of his wages shall be supplied with a reasonable
quantity of Fire Coal paying the said Owner 3d per week for leading
the same. THIRD – The said owners shall provide at each pit a tub to
contain 87.249 imperial Gall. which shall be equivalent to a 20 peck
Corf or a weighing machine: in which case the coals to be 6 cwt and
30   whenever any corves shall be sent to bank suspected to be deficient in
measure of weight the coals therein shall be measured or weighed by
the heap keeper . . . and if found deficient, no payment shall be made
for the hewing and filling the same but the hewer hereof shall not be
subject to any forfeiture or penalty on that account, neither shall any
35   payment be made for hewing and filling any corf in which shall be
found stone or splint to the amount of 1 quart or in Separation
working, in case round coal shall be mixt with small.
         Quoted in B. Lewis, *Coal Mining in the Eighteenth and
         Nineteenth Centuries* (Longman, 1971)

Questions

a   Why did some miners subscribe a mark (line 3)?
b   For how long was the contract of work quoted above legally
     binding?
c   Do you think that the measurements of production laid down,

upon which pay was calculated, were likely to produce dispute?

d   Do you think it was sensible to offer different rates of pay for working the various seams?

e   Do you think the agreement was weighted in the coal owner's favour?

f   Was a fine of 2s 6d a significant penalty (line 23)?

g   From this extract can you see reasons for the growth of miners' grievances?

8   'They Shied Away From General Legislation'

The major areas of affliction (the increasing employment underground of women and children, long hours and insufficient safety regulations) (went) unreported and neglected. This was partly because of the absence of a parliamentary lobby interested in the
5   social welfare of mining communities, for at the beginning of the century miners lacked an effective advocate who, having an intimate knowledge of the industry, could call for improved working conditions. There was no Peel senior, Oastler, Sadler or Fielden, and, although it is true that John Buddle and others were concerned
10   about safety regulations and ventilation, they shied away from general legislation. The Sunderland Society thought that its work was done when Davy presented his lamp, and thereafter went into voluntary liquidation. The terms of its foundation had been narrow and it was not concerned with wider social problems. In its
15   narrowness it represented typical attitudes which persisted among many coal-owners. For although these men were not dyed-in-the-wool villains who lacked common decency (indeed many were genuine philanthropists) they could not believe that there were general rules of conduct which would govern the workings of an
20   efficient coal-mining industry.

Ibid, p 56

Questions

a   What were the main causes of concern in the working of British collieries?

★   b   What is a 'parliamentary lobby' (line 4)?

c   Did Peel senior, Oastler, Sadler and Fielden all have 'intimate knowledge' of any industry (lines 6–7)?

d   Why could coal-owners not 'believe that there were general rules of conduct' that could be enforced in efficient mines (lines 18–19)?

★   e   What was remarkable about Davy's lamp? How did it work?

9   One Man's Wilfulness

Mr Buddle, who was an eye-witness of this explosion, and who cited it to the Lord's Committee in 1829 (Report, p 49) as a marked instance of one man's wilfulness causing the destruction of a large number of his fellow-workmen, gives the following account of it,
5   (1835 Report, 2955–87):
There was a very decent man, his comrade, working in the same place with him; the overman went in with them in the morning and showed them the danger; for although there was no gas in the place they were working in, at about 12 yards from them, in what we call
10   the *return* from the place, which is the way the current of air was going, he actually took them in and showed them that it was explosive. He cautioned them by no means to expose a naked light, inasmuch as they were subject to the operation of what we call backing of the foulness, against the current of air upon their lights.
15   He gave them this caution and went about his business. When this headstrong fellow told his comrade that he could not see with that thing, meaning the Davy, and would insist on screwing off the gauze cylinder and taking his candle, the other remonstrated with him, told him he was aware of the dangers, and he really durst not stop if
20   he persisted in unscrewing the Davy . . . after two or three attempts at the lamp, he obstinately took off the top of it . . . . The other man was so sensible of the danger that he immediately went away . . . he came up the pit, and in a very few minutes the explosion happened . . . . It was a most curious phenomenon . . . an immense
25   cloud immediately over the pit, with a narrow stalk to it, the diameter of the shaft.
Quoted in R. L. Galloway, *Annals of Coal Mining and the Coal Trades*, vol I (David and Charles reprint, 1971), pp 492–3

Questions

★   a   What was John Buddle's contribution to mine safety (line 1)?
★   b   How was the ventilation of a mine usually organised before the invention of mechanical methods?
c   Explain how the 'backing of the foulness' made the working position of the two men dangerous (line 14)?
d   Why was the 'headstrong fellow' so anxious to improve the lighting at the coal face (line 16)?
e   What would cause the Davy lamp's light to dim?
f   What regulations and rules would you recommend as the result of this disaster?

10   Female Work Prohibited

It shall not be lawful for any Owner of any Mine or Colliery whatsoever to employ any Female Person within any Mine or Colliery.

ii . . . it shall not be lawful for any Owner of any Mine or Colliery to employ any Male Person under the Age of Ten Years within any Mine or Colliery.

iii . . . it shall be lawful for One of Her Majesty's Principal Secretaries of State, if and when he shall think fit, to appoint any proper Person or Persons to visit and inspect any Mine or Colliery.

viii . . . where there shall be any Entrance to a Mine or Colliery by means of a vertical Shaft or Pit or Inclined Plane . . . it shall not be lawful for any Owner . . . to allow any Person or Persons other than a Male of the Age of Fifteen Years and upwards to have charge of any Steam Engine or other Engine . . . or to have charge of any Part of the Machinery, Ropes, Chains, or other Tackle of any such Engine, by or by means of which Engine, Machinery, Ropes, Chains or other Tackle Persons are brought up or passed any such Shaft etc.

(Proprietors of Mines, etc. not to pay Wages at Public Houses, etc.)

An Act to prohibit the Employment of Women and Girls in Mines and Collieries, to regulate the Employment of boys etc., 5 and 6 Vict, c. XCiX (99), 10 August 1842

Questions

a What restrictions were imposed upon female, child and juvenile work in mines?
b Do you think that a powerful inspectorate was considered necessary for the mines?
c Why were the mines inspectors not given the power of factory inspectors?
d Do you think the age restriction on winding boys was reasonable?
e Why were coal-owners prohibited from paying wages in such places as public houses?

11 Mining Law Strengthened

I. It shall not be lawful for the Owner of any Mine or Colliery to employ any Male Person under the Age of Twelve years.

II. A Boy above the Age of Ten Years and under the Age of Twelve Years may be employed in a Mine or Colliery (if) such boy is able to read and write.

IV. (Steam Engines in certain cases not to be under the Charge of Persons under 18.)

X. The following Rules (hereinafter referred to as the General Rules) shall be observed in every Colliery or Coal Mine.

10   1. An adequate Amount of Ventilation shall be constantly
         produced in all Coal Mines or Collieries and Ironstone Mines
         to dilute and render harmless noxious gases . . . .
      2. All Entrances to any Place not in actual course of working shall
         be properly fenced off . . . .
15   3. Whenever Safety Lamps are required to be used, they shall be
         first examined and securely locked by a Person . . . duly
         authorised for this Purpose.
      6. Every working Pit or Shaft where the natural strata . . . are not
         safe, shall be securely cased or lined . . . .
20   7. Every working Pit . . . shall be provided with some proper
         Means of Communicating distinct and definite signals for the
         Bottom of Shaft to the Surface.

      XI. In addition to the General Rules, there shall be established and
      observed in every Coal Mine (etc) . . . (Special Rules) . . . as . . .
25   may appear best calculated to prevent dangerous Accidents.
      XVIII. (Owners of Mines to produce Maps or Plans of Mines.)
      XIX. (Notice of Accidents in Mines to be given to Secretary of
      State.)
      XXVII. Every Inspector shall . . . every Year make a . . . Report.
30   XXVIII. The wages of each and every Person employed in any
      Coal Mine . . . shall be paid . . . in money.
      XXIX. Where the Persons employed in any Coal Mine (etc) are
      paid by the Weight, Measure or Gauge of the Coal, Ironstone, or
      other material gotten by them, such Coal (etc) . . . shall be truly
35   weighed, measured or gauged accordingly; and it shall be lawful for
      such Persons, at their own Cost, to station a Person being One of the
      Persons for the Time being employed in such Coal Mine . . . at the
      Place appointed for such weighing . . . in order to take an account
      thereof.
         An Act for the Regulation and Inspection of Mines, 28
         August 1860

Questions

   a What do you think was the effect upon families in coal-mining
      areas of Clause II?
   b What earlier enactment did Clause IV amend?
   c What is the purpose of the third general rule?
   d Of what benefit could the seventh general rule be?
   e How did Clauses XVIII, XIX and XXVII help to improve mine
      safety generally?
   f Why did wages have to be paid in money (Clause XXVIII)?
   g Who paid the checkweighman in Clause XXIX?
   h What kind of man had to be selected as checkweighman?
   i Why could the checkweighman prove influential?
★ j What longstanding grievances did Clause XXIX remedy?

12 Competent Managers

26. Every Mine to which this Act applies shall be under the control
and daily supervision of a manager, and the owner or agent of every
such mine shall nominate himself or some other person . . . to be the
manager.
5   A person shall not be qualified to be a manager of a mine to which
this Act applies unless he is for the time being registered as the holder
of a certificate under this Act.
     27. For the purpose of granting . . . certificates of competency to
managers of mines . . . examiners shall be appointed by a board
10   constituted as hereinafter mentioned.
          An Act to consolidate and amend the Acts relating to the
          Regulation of Coal Mines and certain other Mines (1872)

Questions

a What is the effect of Clauses 26 and 27 taken together?
b Was the state the best source of authentication of certificates of
   competency for mine managers?
★ c What developments in mine engineering made it increasingly
   important for managers to be technically qualified?

13 Common Standards throughout the Industry

(a) A workman shall not be below ground in a mine for the purpose
of his work, and of going to and from his work, for more than eight
hours during any consecutive twenty-four hours.
          Coal Mines Regulation Act, 1908

(b) 1. (1) It shall be an implied term of every contract for the
5 employment of a workman underground in a coal mine that the
employer shall pay to that workman wages at not less than the
minimum rate settled under this Act and applicable to that
workman.
          Coal Mines (Minimum Wage) Act, 1912

Questions

a Could face workers expect to be at their place of work or in
   activities associated with their employment for more than 8
   hours after 1908? If so, what would they be doing?
b Which miners gained most from the establishment of a minimum
   wage?
c Why was the principle of a minimum wage likely to benefit all
   miners?

VI Public Health and the Sanitary Principle

Introduction

Before the great cholera outbreak in 1866, progress in public health was slow, and, where it occurred at all, piecemeal. The early Victorian approach was fundamentally negative; central government did not attempt to set the pace but rather to provide the powers which others might, if they wished, use. The whole tradition of government was against the positive interference of the central powers. Parliament had plenty of information: select committees and royal commissions as well as private individuals and philanthropic societies poured out their evidence and recommendations. It became clear that appalling conditions were not confined to the industrial towns. As long as political society, however, put property rights almost without qualification, before everything else then it was impossible to overcome the forces of inertia.

There were many reasons why improvement could only come slowly. The growth of towns had not been accompanied by a systematic growth in local government. Ancient rural jurisdictions survived while industrial populations exploded in their areas; at the same time, the municipal corporations were reorganised for greater efficiency and accountability rather than given greater responsibility and power. The initiative, therefore, for improvement came from local areas as contemporary views demanded. Unfortunately since there were no ground rules or framework established by parliament within which local acts were made, there developed a vast number of authorities, each with its own *amour propre*, officials and propertied and legal rights to defend, unrelated and uncoordinated and often conflicting. In such an atmosphere sterile arguments certainly prospered, but the conditions of society remained little changed. It is no surprise that reformers and administrators like Chadwick urged upon parliament the need for wholesale reform of local government.

There were other problems involved in the solution of the massive problems which faced government, central and local. Scientific understanding of problems of public health was far from clear or complete or accurate. Only slowly were the real causes of cholera, tuberculosis and diphtheria revealed; until then efforts were to some degree misdirected by miasma theories. New sciences such as civil engineering were in their infancy; new techniques had to be invented before they could be tried and tested. This was particularly true in solving one fundamental interlinked problem: plentiful supplies of water and water-driven sewerage. Not surprisingly arguments developed over what types of sewers were best. Technology, however, was one problem, finding the necessary funds was another. Expenditure upon the new technologies to cure long-lasting problems was immense. Even with the money, technology and directed will of both central and local government, change took time.

Until there was the fundamental reappraisal of government that was needed, change was doomed to be slender. Chadwick's great hope, the Public Health Act of 1848, in practice was a failure even though it asserted vital principles and the Public Health Board was immensely active. Between 1858 and 1871 the Privy Council and Home Office controlled the local boards of health; vigorous direction was given by Sir John Simon. Reorganisation of responsibilities produced the Local Government Board; at the local level the Public Health Act of 1872 redefined the authorities and the areas in which they had responsibility. Medical officers of health were now compulsory appointments in the local sanitary authorities. Removal of nuisances was made enforceable from 1866 and the Public Health Act 1875 covered a vast area of public health from water supply and sewage removal to food inspection and the regulation of markets.

As public expectations changed from the least government possible to positive interference, new authorities, counties, county boroughs, urban and rural districts took over concern for public health. The most important concern they had to face was housing: overcrowded and insanitary accommodation was one of the principal causes of illness. The Housing of the Working Classes Acts of 1890 and 1900 gave local authorities powers to purchase compulsorily, to demolish unhealthy buildings and to provide something better. Operation of these acts proved difficult and onerous. Tougher legislation followed in 1909; nonetheless results before the outbreak of the Great War were disappointing.

With the conclusion of peace, the country was faced with a huge shortage of housing, particularly for the lower-paid workers, and a change in expectations; the general hope was not just of more houses but of better designed, more comfortable and convenient homes. To satisfy this hope, a new policy of state-aided housing was begun. This policy was incorporated in the Housing Act of 1919 and was continued in the legislation of 1923 and 1924. At the same time acts in 1930, 1933 and 1935 were produced to continue the attack on slum clearance and overcrowding. The cost was considerable: £2,500 million was invested in housing between 1920 and 1938; the benefit, commensurate, at least.

1 'Picturesquely situated in a Grove of Trees'

It was a compact city (Exeter in 1800), picturesquely situated in a grove of trees, its open fields occupied by 'racks' for stretching and drying the newly washed, cleaned and dyed serges. The city itself, almost confined within its original walled boundaries, was divided
5   tolerably equally into four parts (by its roads) . . . the streets were generally narrow, and the city abounded in courts, lanes and alleys; it was almost entirely paved with round stones, which pavement was locally known by the name of 'pitching'; this usually ran in declivities from the sides towards the centre, so that in the middle of
10   the road was usually seen the gutter, which conveyed away all the nuisance of the city. . . . But the state of the city is yet more strongly marked . . . (in) that so late as 1808, there was but one water-closet in the city, and that emptied itself into the open street; that it was then the practice for the inhabitants to have tub receptacles within
15   their own houses for the reception of the necessary filth, and which, as occasion required, were towards evening, carried through the streets in order to be emptied into the river . . . the city depended almost entirely for its supply of water on the ordinary sources of rain, springs, and sunken wells, on the conduit (which brought into
20   the city from the east) and the river.

> Report on the Sanitary Condition of Exeter by Thomas Shapter M.D., pp 350–80

> Appendix, Second Report of the Commissioners of Inquiry into the State of Large Towns and Populous Districts, 1845 (602), XVIII

Questions

a What did Exeter manufacture in 1800?
b Had it expanded very much in recent years?
c What were the main methods of refuse and sewage disposal?
d What were the methods of water supply in the city? Which do you think was the safest and the most dangerous source of water supply?
e Why was 'pitching' an unsatisfactory method of street paving?
f What feature of the city in 1800 would have most impressed a modern visitor?

2 Social Change and Urban Decay

In 1800 (the parish of) St. Mary Major contained a population of

2,135, including, together with the poor, a large proportion of respectable people; the houses were ample; containing on the average each 1.84 families and 7.14 persons; it was in fact then far
5   from a very poor parish. In 1831, its population had increased to 3,516, and with this its wealth and respectability had decreased, in fact now inhabited chiefly by poor if not paupers. The houses had become more densely peopled, containing on an average more than two (2.11) families and nine individuals to each. With regard to
10 drainage and the supply of water, much the same condition prevailed at both periods.

Table XIII

There are living out of every
hundred who die:

At Years of Age	In 1800	In 1831
10	52.05	50.23
20	48.52	45.33
30	42.32	40.86
40	37.59	33.55
50	30.12	28.00
60	23.02	20.25
70	15.01	11.31
80	4.44	4.77
90	0.40	0.29

On looking at these tables . . . we find in the latter and worse periods of the parish, both the deaths per cent and the deaths at different ages characterise it as liable to a much higher rate of mortality than in
15 1800; that the mortality is greater by a very considerable amount in the earlier periods of life . . . so that we have here a very strong and remarkable confirmation of the deduction that the chief sources of excessive mortality are the crowding together masses of population into situations ill-ventilated, ill-drained and badly supplied with
20 water.

Report on the Sanitary Condition of Exeter by Thomas Shapter M.D., pp 350–80

Appendix, Second Report of the Commissioners of Inquiry into the State of Large Towns and Populous Districts, 1845 (602), XVIII

Questions

a   By what amount and percentage had the population of the parish grown in thirty years?

b What change had occurred in the character of the people who lived in the area?
c Did it have a 'much higher rate of mortality' in 1831 (line 14)?
d Was mortality greater in 'earlier periods of life' (line 16)?
e What reasons does Shapter give for the 'excessive mortality' in 1831 (line 18)?
f Do you think his judgement is sound?

3 A Home in the Country

At Stourpain, a village near Blandford, I measured a bedroom in a cottage consisting of two rooms, the bedroom in question upstairs, and a room on the ground-floor in which the family lived during the day. There were eleven in the family: and the aggregate earnings
5 in money were 16s. 6d weekly (December 1842), with certain advantages, the principal being the father's title to a grist of a bushel of corn a week, at 1s. below the market price, his fuel carted for him, etc. They had also an allotment of a quarter of an acre, for which they paid a rent of 7s. 7d a year. The following diagram shows the shape
10 of the room and the position of the three beds, A, B, C, it contained. The room was ten feet square, not reckoning the two small recesses by the sides of the chimney, about 18 inches deep. The roof was the thatch, the middle of the chamber being about seven feet high. Opposite the fire-place was a small window, about 15 inches square,
15 the only one to the room.

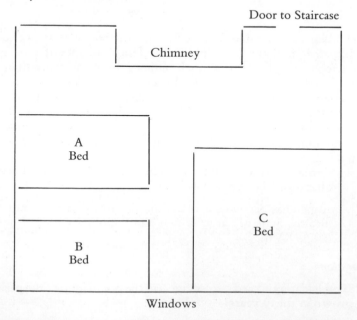

Bed A was occupied by the father and mother, a little boy, Jeremiah, aged 1½ year, and an infant aged 4 months.

Bed B was occupied by the three daughters – the two eldest, Sarah and Elizabeth, twins, aged 20; and Mary, aged 7.

20 Bed C was occupied by the four sons – Silas, aged 17; John, aged 15; James, aged 14; and Elias, aged 10.

There was no curtain, or any kind of separation between the beds.

This I was told was not an extraordinary case; but that, more or less, every bedroom in the village was crowded with inmates of both 25 sexes, of various ages, and that such a state of things was caused by the want of cottages.

Reports of the Special Assistant Poor Law Commissioners on the Employment of Women and Children in Agriculture, 1843. Mr Austin on the Counties of Wilts, Dorset, Devon and Somerset, pp 19–20

Questions

a What was the total income of the family?
b Do you think that this farm-labouring family was substantially worse off than the cotton-spinning family mentioned in Chapter 1?
c Is it possible that the family could have found it difficult to work the allotment?
d Do you think the ventilation and heating of the bedroom adequate?
e Was the bedroom big enough for the whole family? Was there enough headroom?
f 'The roof was the thatch'; did this bring any problems (lines 12–13)?
g What was the cause of such overcrowding?

4 A Model Cottage

I herewith transmit them to you, and it will be observed that there are three sets, two of two cottages each, and one of four cottages. Without entering into details respecting all the eight, I will draw your attention to the double cottages of 1819. Each of these has a 5 front room, 17 feet by 12 feet in width, and 7 feet to 7 feet 6 inches high; a back kitchen of the same height, and 13 feet by 9 feet wide, together with a pantry on the same floor. Above these are three bedrooms which, in different proportions, cover the space already specified for the ground floor. At a convenient distance behind, each 10 cottage has attached to it a wash-house, a dirt-bin, a privy, and a pig-cot. I may add that the drainage is excellent; that the water is good; that each cottage has about 20 rods of garden-ground, and that the rent, including gardens, is only £3 3s. a year. Hence it is not to be wondered at that Mr Emerson the builder has been enabled to say, in

ELEVATION OF Nº 4 COTTAGES. ERECTED IN 1818.

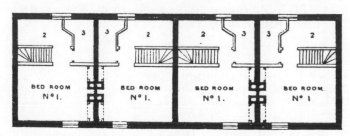

CHAMBER PLAN OF Nº 4 COTTAGES, ERECTED IN 1818.

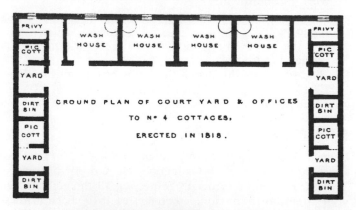

GROUND PLAN OF COURT YARD & OFFICES
TO Nº 4 COTTAGES,
ERECTED IN 1818.

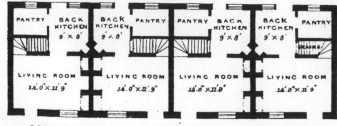

GROUND PLAN Nº 4. COTTAGES, ERECTED IN 1818.

Mr Twisleton's Report on Cottages &c.

COTTAGES BUILT BY THE EARL OF LEICESTER.
AT HOLKHAM. IN NORFOLK.

The Rent for them (including Garden Ground) is 3£ 3s. a year.

ELEVATION Nº2 COTTAGES, ERECTED. 1819.　　　ELEVATION Nº2 COTTAGES, ERECTED 1820.

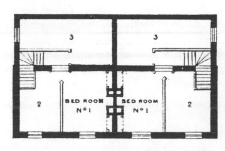
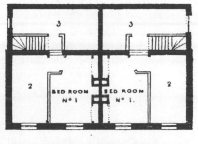

CHAMBER PLAN Nº 2 COTTAGES, 1819.　　　CHAMBER PLAN Nº 2 COTTAGES, 1820.

PLAN OF OFFICES Nº 2 COTTAGES. 1819.　　　PLAN OF OFFICES Nº 2 COTTAGES, 1820.

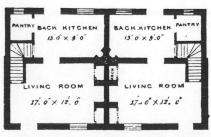
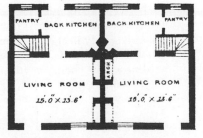

GROUND PLAN Nº 2 COTTAGES, 1819.　　　GROUND PLAN Nº 2 COTTAGES, 1820.

PUBLIC HEALTH AND THE SANITARY PRINCIPLE　　71

15 a letter to me: 'I have never known in them an instance of fever or any
epidemic'.

These cottages are cited as showing what may be done by a landed
proprietor who takes as great a pride in his good cottages and farms
as others in fine hunters and race-horses, rather than with the least
20 intention of asserting that the example is ever likely to be universally
imitated. The cost of building two such cottages is stated by
Emerson to be £220. or £230., which would be £110. or £115. each.
Now, although individuals, here and there, may build cottages
without regard to the pecuniary return, it may be assumed as
25 incontrovertible, that no class of cottages will be universally adopted
which does not command a reasonable interest for the money
expended on them. But considering the cost of repairs and the
frequent trouble and uncertainty of obtaining the rents, it will
probably not be denied that £6. a year would be the minimum as a
30 remunerative rent for the outlay of £110. or £115. on a cottage.
However, the rent of £6. would scarcely be paid by the agricultural
population generally at the present wages: for reckoning the rate of
wages at 12s. a week (which would be high for some parts of the
country), very few would be willing, out of that sum, to expend
35 2s. 3¾d. a week, or nearly a fifth of their earnings, for the rent of
their cottage.

> Local Reports to the Poor Law Commissioners on the
> Sanitary Conditions of the Labouring Population of
> England, 1842 (County of Norfolk)

Questions

a In what ways was the cottage accommodation on the Earl of
Leicester's estate so superior to that at Stourpain?
b Was the rent a major burden for the labourer who occupied the
cottage? How does it compare with the cotton spinner's rent?
(See Chaper 1.)
c How could the farm labourer's family supplement his basic
wage?
d Why was there 'frequent trouble and uncertainty of obtaining the
rents' (line 28)?
e Do you think £6 rent p.a. was reasonable on a building cost of
between £110 and £115?
f Why was the Earl of Leicester's example unlikely 'to be
universally imitated' (lines 20–1)?
g Why was it possible for Mr Emerson to claim that he had 'never
known in them an instance of fever or any epidemic' (lines
15–16)?

5 Overcrowding, a Universal Problem

2343 (Witness) In the year 1831 I was first employed by Mr Watkins the head grave-digger at St. Clement's churchyard.

2348 (Mr Cowper) How long did you work before you were taken ill?

5   I worked there between five and six years before I was taken ill; I was once taken; I got up one Sunday morning and went into the ground in Portugal Street; we had a grave to open; I believe it was 10 feet; I went in and completed the work, and I cut four or five coffins through in that piece of ground, and the bodies of some; I placed the

10   flesh behind and I went home to my breakfast; it was our church time; we did not dare do any more till the people were in church, for the sound of cutting away the wood was so terrible that mobs used to be around the railings and looking . . . .

2351. How many coffins have you dug through, and bodies cut

15   through, to get to a depth of 10 feet?

To get 10 feet of ground you must cut through at least five or six; in the almshouses I could uncover, at least, and expose a dozen coffins within the hour.

2358. How near is the wood of the coffins to the surface?

20   There are coffins now within a foot of the surface.

Minutes of Evidence: Select Committee on Improvement of the Health of Towns: Effect of Interment of Bodies in Towns (1842)

Questions

a   In what kind of graveyard did the witness work?

b   Why was he instructed to dig to a depth of 10 feet?

c   Why did the maintenance of this graveyard cause so much offence to contemporary society?

d   Why was the condition of the graveyard at the almshouses worse?

e   What was the generally accepted explanation of the spread of disease at the time? Why did the gravedigger think he had fallen ill?

f   Given that the Select Committee was concerned with 'the Public Health', what recommendations ought it to have made?

6 'Applicable to towns now, or at any future time'

The first measure they recommend is, a general Building Act, applicable to towns now, or at any future time, comprising a certain amount of population; laying down regulations respecting the

construction of certain rates of houses (well understood among
5 builders) which are fitted for the dwellings of the working classes.

The regulations would be framed so as to interfere no farther with
every one's right to manage his own property than was necessary to
protect the health of the community . . . .

These regulations would forbid and prevent such forms of
10 construction specified, as experience and undoubted testimony
show to be inconsistent with health. These would embrace:

1. Cellar dwellings, unless with areas in front and back, and with
sewers below the level of the floors.

2. Rows of houses erected in close courts, built up at the end.
15 3. Rows of dwellings built back to back, so as to prevent any
through ventilation . . . .

In pursuance of these principles, and with the view of affording to
the poorer classes congregated in towns some protection from the
evils to which, from the confined nature to their dwellings, and the
20 cupidity of speculators, they are frequently exposed, Your
Committee are of the opinion that it would be advisable to establish,
in every town containing a population of a certain amount, a Board
of Health, whose duty it should be to examine into such
circumstances and occurrences within their district as are prejudicial
25 to the general health of the inhabitants . . . . They should also
report their proceedings annually to the Central Board of Health . . .
or to the Secretary of State for the Home Department . . . .

Your Committee have next to suggest that facilities be afforded
for the establishment in towns and newly-extended suburbs of an
30 administrative authority for drainage or sewerage, without the
necessity of incurring the expense and delay of a local Act (i.e. a
General Sewerage Act) . . . .

Your Committee believe it would also be of the greatest
advantage to the inhabitants of great towns if an inspector was
35 appointed to enforce the due execution of sanatory regulations.

Viewing, therefore, the necessity and advantage of such local
improvements, and the difficulties which now prevent them, Your
Committee beg to recommend the introduction of a general Act . . .
to facilitate such improvements.

Report of the Select Committee on the Health of Towns,
1840

Questions

a Why did the Committee recommend a 'general Building Act'
(line 1)?
b What rights had to be preserved while the public interest was
pursued?
c What types of building would the Committee have prohibited?
d What were the evils to which the poorer classes were 'frequently
exposed' (line 20)?

e Why would the appointment of an inspector be 'of the greatest advantage' (lines 33–4)?

★ *f* Why had legislation affecting public health been purely local in character?

★ *g* What advantages could general acts give that local acts could not?

h What other general acts, and for what reasons, did the Committee recommend?

i What, in the Committee's view, should be the functions of the local Board of Health?

j What was the value of a Central Board of Health?

7 Resistance to Reform (1)

37.

In 1841 the Exeter Water Company laid 4-inch main pipes along all the three streets of St. Thomas. They allow to each customer 40 feet of ½-inch service-pipe, and a ball and stop-cock. The service-pipe outside the premises they keep in repair; inside, though the pipe is
5 fixed by the Company, the repairs are borne by the consumer. The water is always on, at a very considerable pressure. It is at present unfiltered, and sometimes turbid; a sample taken from the tap was only of 3° of hardness. The annual charge for the poorest house is 5s. The company entered St. Thomas under an expectation held out by
10 certain parishioners that the demand would be considerable; it has in reality been very trifling. They supply only 47 families, of which only 10 inhabit the cottage class of houses. The gross annual revenue derived from this district is only £101.2s., of which only £34.10s. is from domestic supply. The rest is paid by large consumers, public
15 establishments, and for watering the roads in summer.

38.

The proceedings of the Water Company in St. Thomas are decidedly liberal. Their allowance for service-piping is, on an average, sufficient and their water needs only filtering to be of the finest quality. The quantity they allow is unlimited, and given continually,
20 and yet only about 245 persons, or about 5.7% of the population, and of these only 50 of the poorer classes, or 1.1% of the population, profit directly and legitimately by the supply.

39.

The causes of this indisposition to profit by so great a boon appear to be, in a small degree, the objection on the part of the landlord to
25 incur any expense that he is not forced to do, even though so trifling as that required to maintain the house service pipes in repair, and in

some degree the want of house-drainage, without which a regular supply would often be a great inconvenience.

> Report to the General Board of Health on a Preliminary Enquiry into the Sewerage, Drainage, and Supply of Water, and the Sanitary Condition of the Inhabitants of the Parish of St Thomas the Apostle in the County of Devon, by George T. Clark, Superintending Inspector, 1849

Questions

a Why could it be said that the proceedings of the Water Company 'are decidedly liberal' (lines 16–17)?
b Who were the principal consumers of water in the district?
c Why was it necessary to water the roads in summer?
d Was the cost of piped water within the capacity of the poorer classes to pay?
e What prevented more houses taking advantage of the piped supply?
f Why was it said that the water was nearly of 'the finest quality' (lines 18–19)?

8 Resistance to Reform (2)

(a) The first and undoubtedly greatest objection to the Board of Health is the deserved unpopularity of two of its members; the second, the vice of its constitution by which those members are empowered to carry out their perverse will, their petty intrigues and
5 their wrong-headed dogmatism without restraint and without responsibility. Mr Chadwick and Dr Southwood Smith are just such men as always arise when a dynasty, a Ministry, or a Board is accumulating those elements of destruction of which it alone is unconscious. Possessing faculties by no means miraculously
10 comprehensive, engaged upon, and brought in contact with many honest prejudices and much not unreasonable scepticism, these men seem heated with all the zeal of propagandists and all the intolerance of inquisitors. Firmly persuaded of their own infallibility, intolerant of all opposition, utterly careless of the feelings and wishes of the
15 local bodies with whom they are brought in contact, determined not only to have their own way, and using the powers delegated to them to exercise influence over matters which Parliament has placed beyond their control, these gentlemen have contrived to overwhelm a good object with obliquy and hatred and to make the cholera itself
20 scarcely a more dreaded visitation than their own.

> The Times leader, 11 July 1854

(b) We prefer to take our chance of cholera and the rest than be bullied into health

There is nothing a man so hates as being cleansed against his will, or having his floors swept, his walls whitewashed, his pet dungheaps cleared away, or his thatch forced to give way to slate, all at the command of a sort of sanitary bombailiff. It is a positive fact that
25   many have died of a good washing. All this shows the extreme tenderness with which the work of purification should advance. Not so, thought Mr Chadwick. New mops wash clean, thought he, and he set to work, everywhere washing and splashing, and twirling and rinsing, and sponging and sopping, and soaping and mopping, till
30   mankind began to fear a deluge of soap and water. It was a perpetual Saturday night, and Master John Bull was scrubbed, and rubbed, and small-tooth-combed, till the tears came into his eyes, and his teeth chattered, and his fists clinched themselves with worry and pain. The truth is, Mr Chadwick has very great powers, but it is not
35   so easy to say what they can be applied to. Perhaps a retiring pension, with nothing to do, will be a less exceptionable mode of rewarding this gentleman, than what is called an active sphere.

The Times, July 1854 quoted in R. Watson, *Edwin Chadwick, Poor Law and Public Health* (Longman, 1969)

Questions

a   What is meant by the 'wrong-headed dogmatism' of Chadwick and Southwood Smith (line 5)?
b   With what offence are they accused in lines 17–18?
c   What was there in the methods, as well as the powers entrusted to the Board of Health, to which *The Times* objected?
d   What principle was *The Times* determined to defend?
e   Was 'The Thunderer' worthy of its appellation?

9   A Good System of Government?

1650
You are aware that there is a deficiency of those regulations (concerning drainage, sewerage and cleansing) in many of the large towns? –
There is a deficiency both of the powers to be exercised and of
5   proper authorities to exercise them.

1651
Will you be kind enough to point out the deficiencies you consider there are, first of all in the powers, and next, in the authorities requisite for the purpose of putting them into action where they are already in existence; first of all, with respect to the powers in places
10   in the neighbourhood of London? –

In the metropolis the committee are aware of the constitution and powers of the various Boards of Sewers. But the municipal system of London, if system it can be called, is exceedingly intricate; the old corporation of the city presides over only about 250,000 inhabitants
15   out of the whole metropolis; their powers are very various; and even in the city of London the sewers are vested in a distinct corporation, and there are several other bodies in the city who have their peculiar portions of municipal administration. Out of the city of London, independently of various Commissions of Sewers, there are
20   municipal bodies of great variety, both in their purposes and in their constitution; these have never been the subject of any investigation, so that I cannot state minutely what they are; but in the borough of Mary-le-bone, for instance, the number of Boards to whom the paving and lighting, and the cleansing of the streets is variously
25   entrusted is quite surprising; and the number of local Acts is not less than 80.

1652
With respect to the powers of ventilation, cleansing and sewerage on the other large towns, will you have the goodness to state the information you possess? –
30   The powers possessed by the authorities in whom they are vested are exceedingly various; they form no system and never have formed a system. The old bodies, in whom all municipal powers were vested, were either the corporations of the towns, or the manorial jurisdictions of the country; under some of the manorial jurisdictions
35   have accumulated large manufacturing populations, forming now some of the largest towns in the kingdom; such as Manchester, Birmingham, Bolton, and several of the large towns of Yorkshire. Other towns possessing ancient municipal constitutions have also some of them grown up to be places of immense size, such as
40   Liverpool. Under the recent Act for the Amendment of Municipal Corporations, all those towns which had the old municipal constitutions have received something that may be called a municipal system; the constitutions of all of them are now similar. When I say the powers of all of them are alike, it is with this
45   exception, that the Act, though it gives to all those municipal bodies a power to receive, yet it confers on none a power to demand the authorities now exercised by the co-existent Boards under local Acts.

1654
The local Acts which have been obtained in various of those
50   populous towns are different from each other in power and extent? –
They are.

1655
Are they also in many instances unequal to the objects for which they
were obtained? –

In a great many instances; with regard to the constitution of the
55 local Boards which they erect, they are various, from the
circumstances under which they have been passed. As large
populations have accumulated, some sort of municipal regulation
has been found absolutely necessary, and part of the inhabitants,
whichever party was the strongest, or whichever party in the town
60 thought it right to try first for an Act, would form a plan among
themselves according to their local interests and feelings; the party
which is this way reduced into form the plan, brought it to the House
of Commons; a measure not made by the House on any system, but
made in the country, under the influence of local feelings and
65 purposes of the parties themselves, without control or direction.
The House of Commons rather registered their enactments than
formed a municipal constitution upon any system; the consequence
is, that the territorial extent of the jurisdiction of these commissions
under local Acts is often exceedingly arbitrary, and it may be said, in
70 some instances, perfectly absurd; for they include, perhaps, only the
centre of a town, or but parts of its suburbs, or only half a town;
or there will be three or four commissions existing
contemporaneously. [Here he cites the instance of Wakefield, 11
Geo. III, c. 44.]

Minutes of Evidence, Select Committee on the Health of
Towns, 1840. Witness: Mr Joseph Fletcher

Questions

a   How many types of municipal administration are mentioned in
this extract?
b   What were 'manorial jurisdictions' (line 34)?
c   Was there a good case to be made for treating London separately
from the rest of the country?
d   Why did the large industrial towns mentioned lack the necessary
powers to deal with their problems?
e   What was the great weakness of the reformed corporations?
f   What kind of organisation was the witness describing in answer
1655?
g   Why were local acts sometimes 'perfectly absurd' (line 70)?
h   Why were these various local authorities likely to resent
centralised state power?
i   Do you think this great variety in administration helped or
hindered improvement?

10 The Enjoyment of a Warm Bath

In a very short manner was stated the great inconvenience which a
poor family occupying . . . only one room, were obliged to submit
to, from the necessity they were under of their washing being carried
on in the same room, where, perhaps, there is a mother who has just
5   laid in, or a sick person who required the greatest attention, or even a
dying person . . . . There were no conveniences for ironing or
drying . . . . As to the advantage of establishing wash-houses for
the poor, he did not anticipate there was the slightest difference of
opinion. With respect to baths for the use of the poor, he had heard
10   objections . . . . Again he had heard it said – there was the river –
people may go and bathe in the river . . . . Some gentlemen referred
to their schooldays when they used to go down and bathe . . . and
run about naked in the meadows to dry themselves. This might be a
very proper amusement for little boys, but they would not approve
15   of great, strong stalwart working artificers running by dozens naked
about the fields in that sort of way. . . . there were but three months
in which to enjoy the luxury of a river bath, whilst it was desirable
they should enjoy throughout the year – (Cheers).

    The Dean of Exeter appealing for public subscriptions to
build public baths and wash-houses for the poor of Exeter.
Report in *Exeter Flying Post*, 10 January 1850

Questions

a   What advantages does the Dean think will accrue from the
provision of such public facilities recommended under the Baths
and Wash-houses Act, 1846?
b   Does the Dean really understand the problems involved in
provision for the poor?
c   What dangers were presented by river bathing?

11 The Board of Health

iv. The First Commissioner . . . of Her Majesty's Woods and
Forests . . . together with Two other Persons . . . shall be and
constitute a Board for superintending the Execution of this Act, and
shall be called "The General Board of Health".
5   vi. The General Board of Health may . . . appoint so many
proper Persons . . . to be superintending Inspectors.
   xii. In every District exclusively consisting the whole or Part of
One Corporate Borough the Mayor, Aldermen and Burgers . . .
shall be . . . for such District the local Board of Health.
10   xxxviii. The local Board of Health shall from Time to Time
appoint Fit and Proper Persons to be Surveyors, Inspectors of
Nuisances, Clerk and Treasurer.

xl. The local Board of Health may . . . appoint the Officer of Health.
> Public Health Act, 1848

Questions

a To what organisation was the Board of Health similar?
b What was likely to be the function of the Inspectors?
c The Act required the appointment of Inspectors of Nuisances but did not require that of Officers of Health; can you explain the reasoning here?
★ d Who was the driving force behind the Act and the Board?
★ e Why did the Board have such a short life?

12 Local Boards Develop Greater Powers

xxxii. Local Boards may themselves undertake or contract with any Persons for:
> The proper Cleansing and Watering of Streets
> The Removal of House Refuse from Premises
5 The Cleansing of Privies, Ashpits and Cesspools.
xxxiv. Every local Board may make Bye-laws with respect to the following Matters:
19. With respect to the Level, Width and Construction of new Streets and the Provisions of the Sewerage thereof.
10 With respect to the Structure of Walls of new Buildings for securing Stability and the Prevention of Fires.
With respect to the Sufficiency of the Space about Buildings to secure a free Circulation of Air.
With respect to the Drainage of Buildings.
15 liii. It shall be lawful for any Local Board of Health absolutely to purchase, and for the Directors for the Time being of any Waterworks Company or Market Company, . . . to sell convey and transfer unto any Local Board of Health . . . all the Rights, Powers (etc) of the Company.
> Local Government Act, 1858

Questions

a Under what conditions was clause xxxii likely to prove valuable?
b Why was it so important to have such regulations for new streets (clause xxxiv)?
c Why was the Act so concerned about the free circulation of air?
d What was the weakness of clause liii?

13   The Duties of Local Authorities

91. Nuisances. For the purpose of this act,

1. Any premises in such a state as to be a nuisance or injurious to health;
2. Any pool ditch gutter watercourse privy urinal cesspool drain or
5   ashpit so foul or in such a state as to be a nuisance (etc);
3. Any animal so kept as to be a nuisance (etc);
4. Any accumulation or deposit which is a nuisance . . . .
5. Any house or part of a house so overcrowded as to be dangerous or injurious to the health of the inmates;
10   6. Any factory workshop or workplace . . . not kept in a cleanly state, nor ventilated in such manner as to render harmless . . . any gases vapours dust etc . . . that are a nuisance or injurious to health;
7. Any fireplace or furnace which does not as far as practicable consume the smoke arising from the combustible used therein . . .
15   shall be deemed nuisances liable to be dealt with summarily in manner provided in this Act.

92. It shall be the duty of every local authority to be caused to be made from time to time inspection of their district . . . to ascertain what nuisances exist . . . in order to abate the same.
        Public Health Act, 1875

Questions

a   What does Clause 91 achieve?
b   What does Clause 92 require?
c   How is Clause 92 different from the Public Health Act, 1848, and the Local Government Act, 1858?

14   Schemes of Improvement

Part I. Unhealthy areas.
        3. Where an official representation . . . is made to the local authority that any houses, courts or alleys within a certain area . . . are unfit for human habitation . . . and the sanitary defects in such
5   area cannot be effectually remedied otherwise than by an improvement scheme for the rearrangement and reconstruction of the streets and houses within such area . . . the local authority . . . shall forthwith proceed to make a scheme for the improvement of such area.·
10   5. The improvement scheme of a local authority shall be accompanied by maps, particulars and estimates; it may . . . include any neighbouring lands, if . . . necessary for making their scheme efficient for sanitary purposes; it may also provide for widening any existing approaches to the unhealthy area . . . for the purposes of
15   ventilation or health; also it shall distinguish the lands proposed to be taken compulsorily, and shall provide for the accommodation of at

least as many persons of the working class as may be displaced . . .
unless there are special reasons to the contrary . . . . It may also
provide for such scheme . . . being carried out . . . by the person
20 entitled to the first estate of freehold, . . . or with the concurrence of
such person . . . upon such terms and conditions to be embodied in
the scheme as may be agreed upon between the local authority and
such person.

Artisans' and Labourers' Dwellings Improvement Act, 1875

Questions

a Who do you consider might constitute 'an official representation'
(line 2)?
b In what way does Clause 3 extend the responsibilities of the local
authority?
c Upon what grounds might land and property be purchased
compulsorily?
d Why was it unlikely that rebuilt areas could accommodate as
many as in the past?
e Why do you think the Act provided for the participation of the
freeholder in the improvements?
f Why were local authorities sometimes unwilling to proceed with
such schemes?

15 Compulsion from the Centre

11(1) Where it appears to the Local Government Board that a local
authority have failed to perform their duty under the Housing Acts
of carrying out an improvement scheme . . . or have failed to cause
to be made the inspection of their district required by this Act, the
5 board may make an order requiring the local authority to remedy the
default and to carry out any works . . . which are necessary for the
purpose under the Housing Act within a time fixed by the order.

(2) Any order made by the Local Government Board under this
section may be enforced by a mandamus . . . .

10 Part II Town Planning

54(1) A town planning scheme may be made in accordance with . . .
this Act . . . with the general object of securing proper sanitary
conditions, amenity, and convenience.

57(1) The responsible authority may . . .

15 (a) remove, pull down, or alter any building or work in the area included
in the scheme which is such as to contravene the scheme, or in the erection
or carrying out of which any provision of the scheme has not been
complied with,
or

20   (b) execute any work which it is the duty of any person to execute under the scheme in any case where . . . delay . . . would prejudice the efficient operation of the scheme.

58(1) Any person whose property is injuriously affected by the making of a town-planning scheme shall . . . be entitled to claim
25   compensation.

(2) Where . . . any property is increased in value, the responsible authority . . . shall be entitled to recover . . . one half of that increase.

Housing and Town Planning Act, 1909

Questions

a   What does Clause 11(1) give the Local Government Board the power to do?

b   Can you think of any reasons why local authorities had been failing in their responsibilities?

★ c   What is meant by the enforcement of the Local Government Board's will by a 'mandamus' (line 9)?

d   What is the purpose of Town Planning schemes?

e   What powers were granted to local authorities in Clause 57?

f   How are landlord's rights safeguarded in Clause 58(1)?

g   Whose rights are protected by paragraph 2 of Clause 58?

h   Consider the phraseology of extracts 12, 14, 15. How far does this phraseology illustrate the change of emphasis in legislation over the last 30 or so years of the nineteenth century?

16   Housing (Additional Powers) Act, 1919

1(1) The Minister of Health may . . . make grants out of moneys provided by Parliament to any persons or bodies of persons constructing houses.

(2) Grants under this section shall be made only in respect of
5 houses

(a) which comply with the conditions prescribed by the Minister and are in material accordance with the conditions as to the number of houses per acre and the standards of structural stability and sanitation approved by the Minister . . . ;
10 (b) which are certificated by the local authority . . . to have been completed in a proper and workmanlike manner;
(c) the construction of which is begun within twelve months.

Questions

a   How is this Act different from all previous housing and public health acts?

b   Under what terms would housing grants be made 'to any persons or bodies of persons' (line 2)?

★ c   Is the date of the passage of the Act significant?

VII The Spread of Enlightenment

Introduction

Early in the nineteenth century new types of school founded by the Anglican National Society and the nonconformist British and Foreign Bible Society joined the dames schools and charity schools which served the less well advantaged classes in society. Parents with greater wealth were able to take advantage of the endowed grammar schools or the public schools. The new voluntary schools pioneered by Bell and Lancaster were based on the monitorial system in which the teachers taught monitors and monitors taught children. Between 1809 and 1845 22 church colleges were established to train teachers in such methods.

This pioneering fitted in well with contemporary notions of individualism and private enterprise. Between 1830 and 1870 the attitude towards education changed; it could be claimed that ignorance, no less than poverty and ill-health, prevented the individual from achieving his own fulfilment. That barrier had to be broken down. The voluntary societies were therefore encouraged by state aid. Furthermore two other types of school developed at the same time, pauper schools set up under the Poor Law and schools provided by industry because of the Factory Acts.

These developments were accompanied by a growth in administration, firstly by an Inspectorate and then by the Committee of Privy Council for Education. From 1839 the Committee supervised the grants made to the National Society and the British and Foreign Bible Society. The Inspectors reported to the Committee upon the use made of the money and the quality and quantity of education provided. Behind these developments the emphasis given by statesmen, administrators and politicians was moral: an educated person will be rescued from the possibilities of a life of crime, immorality and disorder and directed into the paths of hard work and thrift. One of the most outstanding inspectors was Matthew Arnold, poet and critic, son of Thomas Arnold, Headmaster of Rugby.

The Newcastle Commission, having investigated the state of popular education, revealed in 1861 that while 2½ million pupils were registered on school rolls and only 4 per cent of the poorer children were receiving no education, a more efficient administration was needed. The result was the Revised Code, a thoroughly Benthamite device.

On the one hand development was impaired by the intense religious argument which developed in the 1840s over educational provisions for the factory children. The dissenting churches, freed from their political disabilities since 1827–29, sought parity with the Established Church. On the other hand greater efficiency and proper purpose was required of the oldest educational foundations in the realm, the Universities of Oxford and Cambridge, the public schools and the endowed schools.

The Education Act of 1870 was of a quite different temper from earlier legislation: the state asserted the need for its positive interference. In part the initiative sprang from awareness of the challenges to Britain's industrial supremacy coming from both Europe and the U.S.A. At first this was confined to 'filling in gaps' but the establishment of the County Councils Act, 1888, the replacement of the Department by the Board of Education and important education acts in 1902 and 1918 helped to bring out a coordinated national system of education.

1 Progress of National Schools

In 1813 (two years after the formation of the society) there were 230 schools in union, containing 40,484 children. In 1817 (when the society was incorporated) the statement made was, schools 725, scholars 117,000; and in 1820 (the period at which the last account
5 was published, previous to that from which this corrected estimate was formed) there were 1,614 schools, and rather more (than) 200,000 scholars. These totals are now, in 1830, carried up to 2,609 places, containing about 3,670 schools, with about 346,000 scholars.

Progress of the Religious Education of the Poor in England and Wales, ascertained from the results of three Inquiries in 1819, 1826 and 1831 (extracted from the Annual Report of the National Society for 1832)

FIRST RESULT IN 1819

Obtained by means of Circulars addressed to the Clergy of the
10 Established Church, by Order of Parliament.

N.B. The Population of England and Wales in the preceding Census of 1811, was 10,150,615.

	ENGLAND				WALES			
	Schools endowed wholly or partially		Unendowed schools		Schools endowed wholly or partially		Unendowed schools	
	Schools	Scholars	Schools	Scholars	Schools	Scholars	Schools	Scholars
On the new System of Mutual Instruction	302	39,590	820	105,582	10	990	41	4,480
Ordinary Schools on the old System	3,865	125,843	10,360	319,643	199	6,635	458	16,873
Endowed Schools	4,167	165,433	11,180	425,225	209	7,625	499	21,353
	—	—	4,167	165,433	—	—	209	7,625
Schools &c. in England			15,347	590,658			708	28,978
							15,347	590,658
Grand Total							16,055	619,636

87

SECOND RESULT IN 1826

Obtained by means of Circulars addressed by the National Society
to the Clergy of the Established Church, under favour of a free cover
granted by His Majesty's Government.

30   N.B. The Population of England and Wales in the preceding
Census of 1821 was 11,978,875.

DIOCESE	Schools	Scholars	DIOCESE	Schools	Scholars
Bangor	46	2248	Lincoln	852	46977
Bristol	213	13921	Lichfield &	574	37098
			Coventry		
Bath & Wells	292	16925	Llandaff	59	2793
Canterbury	227	12992	Norwich	706	32125
Carlisle	79	4056	Oxford	161	7689
Chichester	141	8114	Peterboro'	249	13624
Chester	466	57619	Rochester	80	5610
Durham	167	10133	Salisbury	329	18437
Ely	80	7123	St. David's	136	8431
Exeter	411	23557	St. Asaph	61	3700
Gloucester	274	14312	Winchester	333	21464
Hereford	155	8699	Worcester	170	11308
London	536	34780	York	679	51201
TOTAL	3087	214479	TOTAL	4388	260449
				3087	214479
Returns in which the Schools etc. are accurately given. 410 Schools entered, the Children of which were omitted.				7475	474928
Calculation upon the returns not received				924	55000
			TOTAL	8399	550428

THIRD RESULT IN JANUARY 1832

55   Obtained by means of Circulars as on the National Society's
previous Inquiry in 1826.

N.B. The Population of England and Wales in the Preceding
Census of 1831 was 13,894,574.

N.B. This is the state of education in January 1831; the circulars by
60   which the result was obtained were all dated for the 1st January 1831,
and were issued in December 1830 and January 1831. The Returns in
the Report give the number of schools and scholars etc.

Can you state the present number? The Report now in the press
states the number of places in which there are schools in union with
65   the society at upwards of 3,500, such schools educating above
500,000 children; and, including schools acting upon the same
principle, though not immediately in connexion, 1,000,000 of
children are educating in them.

SUNDAY SCHOOLS

	ENGLAND		WALES	
	Schools	Scholars	Schools	Scholars
On the new System of Mutual Instruction	404	50979	8	713
Ordinary Schools on the old System	4758	401838	283	23695
Total Sunday Schools 5,463; Scholars 477,225	5162	452817	301	24408

Returns presented by William Cotton to parliamentary enquiry (*Parliamentary Papers*, 1834, vol IX, 99, 1876–78), quoted in G. M. Young and W. D. Handcock, *English Historical Documents*, vol XII(1) (1958)

Questions

a How had the number of pupils attending National Schools and those acting on a similar principle changed over the period 1813–32?
b Approximately what proportion of the total population did these 'scholars' represent?
★ c Who developed the National Society?
★ d What were the purposes of the National Society?

2 Dame's Schools: 'Modified black-holes'

The private or 'dame's' schools for the poor are a fruitful source of an injuriously bad atmosphere. The rooms appropriated are usually in crowded and bad situations, small and inhabited by the mistress day and night, with the addition of a fire, winter and summer, for
5 culinary purposes; in an atmosphere thus artificially heated, are congregated together for hours in the day, perhaps 20 children. The closeness and unpleasantness of these rooms is scarcely credible; they may really be termed modified 'black-holes'. The effect upon the children is seen in the breaking down of otherwise strong
10 constitutions, and the development of much active scrofulous disease.

Report on the condition of Exeter by Thomas Shapter, 1845 (602), XVIII, cited in G. M. Young and W. D. Handcock, op cit

Questions

a What were the educational attainments likely to have been of those running such schools?

b Was the atmosphere of such schools likely to assist or impair learning?

c What was the pattern of pupil attendances likely to have been?

3 A 'lamentably deficient' kind of education

Your committee now turn to the state of Education in the large manufacturing and seaport towns, where the population has rapidly increased within the present century; they refer for particulars to the Evidence taken before them, which appears to bear out the

5 following results:

1st. That the kind of education given to the children of the working classes is lamentably deficient.

2nd. That it extends (bad as it is) to but a small proportion of those who ought to receive it.

10 3rd. That without some strenuous and persevering efforts be made on the part of Government, the greatest evils to all classes may follow from this neglect.

Note:

The general result of all these towns is, that about one in 12 receives

15 some sort of daily instruction, but only about one in 24 an education likely to be useful. In Leeds, only one in 41; in Birmingham, one in 38; in Manchester, one in 35.

Your Committee do not propose in this place to enter into more detail on this subject, but refer to the Evidence taken before them;

20 they would especially beg to refer to the Evidence of Dr Kay, Mr Riddall Wood, Mr Corrie, and Mr Buxton. These gentlemen describe in strong terms the misery and crime likely to arise from the neglected education of the children of the working classes in populous places.

25 Your Committee are fully persuaded that to this cause (embracing the want of religious and moral training) is to be chiefly attributed the great increase of criminals and consequently of cost to the country.

With regard to the numbers of children attending Sunday Schools,

30 Your Committee do not think it necessary to enter into any long details, but refer to the Evidence on this point; they consider the instruction there given as of great advantage, by implanting feelings of religion and giving habits of order; but as imperfect without daily instruction also.

Report of the Select Committee on the Education of the Poorer Classes (1837–1838), *Parliamentary Papers*, 1837–38, vol VII, pp vii–ix, quoted in G. M. Young and W. D. Handcock, op cit

	PLACE	Population	Children of working classes at Daily schools, viz.		TOTAL
			Day and Dame schools *Very indifferent*	Other better schools	
40	1836 Liverpool	230,000	11,336	14,024	25,000
	1834 Manchester	200,000	11,520	5,680	17,100
	1835 Salford	50,810	3,340	2,015	5,350
	— Bury	20,000	1,648	803	2,451
45	1835 { Ashton / Duckenfield / Staley Bridge }	47,800	—	—	2,496
	1837 Birmingham	180,000	8,180	4,697	12,877
	1837 Bristol	112,438	} ...not including scholars in private schools ...	5 to 15	4,135
50	1838 Brighton { B. & F.	40,634 in 1831	{ 1,367	Total 3,053	5,254
	National }		863 }	3,247	4,400
	1837 West Bromwich	—	...of 6,375 children under 14 years old	—	4,110
55	1838 Leeds (B. & F.)	123,393 in 1831	...no return of Dame or Day, but only Public schools	2,971	1,554
					—
	1838 Sheffield	96,692 in 1831	3,359	5,905	9,314
60	1838 Northampton { B. & F.	20,000	1,011	1,215	2,226
	National }		996	1,202	2,198
	Reading (B. & F.)	15,595 in 1831	297	962	1,259
	Exeter	28,242 in 1831	2,045	1,830 including evening	3,875
65	1836 York	25,359 in 1831	1,494	2,697	4,191

Questions

a In how many of the towns listed were more children taught in 'other better schools' than in 'very indifferent schools'?
b Do the statistics support the three conclusions of the Report?
c What was the Select Committee's concern in providing education?
d What results, in the Committee's view, had developed because of the lack of schooling?
e What deficiency did the Committee note in the work of the Sunday Schools?

4 The Great Experiment

(a) Mr Baker found the subject, . . . the education state of his district both interesting and painful.

Interesting, because it embraces a subject important to our national prosperity . . . painful, because the experiment . . . is not so
5 satisfactory in its results as it might have been hoped for. Not unsatisfactory as to its practicability . . . but as to the apathy of parents, the laxity of discipline, or want of it in schools and teachers; the non-supervision of schools by local committees and the want of interest and sympathy in the matter of education between the rich
10 and the poor.

As an experiment, compulsory education under the Factory Act has been signally successful . . . thousands of children, now members of various literary and mechanics' institutions have had an education by compulsion . . . who would never have been educated
15 at all.

Report of Mr Saunder for October 1846, *Parliamentary Papers*, 1846, vol XX, p 588

(b)	Boys	Girls	TOTAL
National	2902	1453	4355
British	831	380	1211
Public but not in connexion with the National or British School Societies	1267	753	2020
Factory Schools	2135	1611	3746
Private schools, including Dames Schools	2396	1512	3908
	9531	5709	15240

. . . I am satisfied . . . not more than one third are receiving any education than can have any influence on the formation of their characters, either morally or intellectually. The causes are, indeed, obvious at first sight; the incompetency of the teachers, by reason of
30 their own defective education and their ignorance of the art of conveying instruction to young minds; the miserable supply of books and other materials for teaching and of school furniture; the number of children far exceeding what it is possible even for a highly qualified master to do justice to . . . .
35 Many of the schools established by the owners of factories and printing works . . . are good, some of them excellent; and of the 3746 children in the factory schools, fully a half are as well taught as those in good National and British schools.

Report of L. Horner 1847, *Parliamentary Papers*, 1847, vol XV, p 496

Questions

a What in Horner's view were the causes of so many children receiving only a very poor education?
b Which types of schools were the best in his view?
c Why, in Mr Baker's view, had compulsory education for children not been more successful?
d Why were parents not able to choose the best schools for their children?
e Why was the great 'experiment', as Mr Baker termed it, 'signally successful' (line 12)?

5 Committee of Council for Education

It is some consolation to Her Majesty to perceive that of late years the zeal for popular education has increased, that the Established Church has made great efforts to promote the building of schools, and that the National and British and Foreign School Societies have actively
5 endeavoured to stimulate the liberality of the benevolent and enlightened friends of general Education.

Still much remains to be done; and among the chief defects yet subsisting may be reckoned the insufficient number of qualified schoolmasters, the imperfect mode of teaching which prevails in
10 perhaps the greater number of the schools, the absence of any sufficient inspection of the schools, and examination of the nature of the instruction given, the want of a Model School which might serve for the example of those societies and committees which anxiously seek to improve their own methods of teaching, and, finally, the
15 neglect of this great subject among the enactments of our voluminous Legislation.

Some of these defects appear to admit of an immediate remedy, and I am directed by Her Majesty to desire, in the first place, that your Lordship, with four other of the Queen's Servants, should
20 form a Board or Committee, for the consideration of all matters affecting the Education of the People . . . .

It is proposed that the Board should be entrusted with the application of any sums which may be voted by Parliament for the purposes of Education in England and Wales.

25 Among the first objects to which any grant may be applied will be the establishment of a Normal School.

In such a school a body of schoolmasters may be formed, competent to assume the management of similar institutions in all parts of the country. In such a school likewise the best modes of
30 teaching may be introduced, and those who wish to improve the schools of their neighbourhood may have an opportunity of observing their results.

The Board will consider whether it may not be advisable for some years to apply a sum of money annually in aid of the Normal Schools
35 of the National and of the British and Foreign School Societies.

They will likewise determine whether their measures will allow them to afford gratuities to deserving schoolmasters; there is no class of men whose rewards are so disproportionate to their usefulness to the community.

40 In any Normal or Model School to be established by the Board, four principal objects should be kept in view, viz.

1. Religious Instruction.
2. General Instruction.
3. Moral Training.
45 4. Habits of Industry.

Of these four I need only allude to the first; with respect to Religious Instruction there is, as your Lordship is aware, a wide or apparently wide difference of opinion among those who have been most forward in promoting education . . . .

50 On this subject I need only say that it is Her Majesty's wish that the youth of this kingdom should be religiously brought up, and that the right of conscience should be respected.

Moreover, there is a large class of children who may be fitted to be good members of society without injury or offence to any party – I
55 mean pauper orphans, children deserted by their parents, and the offspring of criminals and their associates.

It is from this class that the thieves and housebreakers of society are continually recruited. It is this class likewise which has filled the workhouses with ignorant and idle inmates.

Lord John Russell's letter to Lord Lansdowne 1839, *Parliamentary Papers*, 1839, vol XLI, pp 255–7, quoted in G. M. Young and W. D. Handcock, op cit

Questions

a What was to be the function of the proposed Committee of Council for Education?

b What deficiencies in providing efficient education did Lord John Russell see?

c What were the objectives of a normal school?

d Why was there a 'wide difference of opinion' over how to provide religious education (line 48)?

e What groups of children could be forcibly educated 'without offence to any party' (line 54)?

f What were the results of the lack of education among the poor?

g Did Lord John Russell consider teachers were well paid?

6 Teacher Apprenticeships

It appeared further expedient to their Lordships, that the Lord President should authorize one or more of Her Majesty's Inspectors, together with the principal of a normal school . . . to submit . . . from among the pupil teachers who had successfully terminated
5 their apprenticeship, a certain number . . . who, upon competition in a public examination . . . might be found most proficient in their studies and skilful in the art of teaching.

That the Committee of Council . . . should award, for as many as they might think fit, an exhibition of £20 or £25 to one of the normal
10 schools.

That the pupil teachers to whom such exhibitions should be awarded should be thenceforward denominated 'Queen's Scholars' . . . .

That it might be useful to offer further incentives to pupil teachers
15 (who) might not display the highest qualifications for the office of schoolmaster, but whose conduct and attainments were satisfactory, an opportunity of obtaining employment in the public service.

In order still further to reduce the burden of such establishments (i.e. normal schools) their Lordships will award to every normal
20 school subject to inspection a grant for every student . . . . Such grants shall be £20 at the close of the first year, £25 at the close of the second and £30 at the close of the third.

Their Lordships will further grant, in aid of the salary of every schoolmaster . . . who has had one year's training in a normal
25 school, £15 or £20 per annum; (or) who has had two years of such training, £20 or £25 per annum (or) who has had three years of such training £25 or £30 per annum . . . on the following conditions:-

1. that . . . the school provide the master with a house rent-free, and a further salary, equal at least to twice the amount of this grant.

30   2. that . . . his character, conduct and attention to his duties are
satisfactory.
        3. that the Inspector report that his school is efficient . . . .
            Parliamentary Papers, 1847, vol XLV, pp 5–6, quoted in
            G. M. Young and W. D. Handcock, op cit

Questions

a   Why did normal schools need financial help in training pupil
    teachers?
b   What do you think were the strengths and weaknesses of such a
    mode of teacher training?
c   Do you think that the scheme had sufficient attraction to
    encourage pupil-teacher performance?
★   d   What alternative methods of teacher training were there?
e   What was proposed for those who failed to show sufficient merit
    in training? Why were such people potentially very valuable?

7   Payment by Results

40. The Managers of Schools may claim at the end of each year . . .
    (a) the sum of 4s. per scholar at morning and afternoon meetings
of their school and 2s. 6d. per scholar . . . at the evening meetings.
    (b) For every scholar who has attended more than 200 morning
5   and afternoon meetings of their schools
    1. if more than six years of age 8s. subject to examination,
    2. if under six years of age 6s. 6d. subject to a report by the
inspector.
    (c) For every scholar who has attended more than 24 evening
10   meetings of their school 5s., subject to examination.
    46. Every scholar for whom grants are claimed must be examined
according to one of the following standards . . . (cont. on p 97)

Questions

a   What kind of behaviour was likely to be encouraged in teachers
    by grants being dependent upon attendances?
b   How would teachers try to attract pupils?
c   Do you think that Matthew Arnold was right when he said that
    the Revised Code gave a 'mechanical turn' to school teaching?
d   Do you think that the principle of payment by results was likely
    to please public opinion in the mid–nineteenth century?
e   What sort of employment would a scholar successfully attaining
    Standard VI have been equipped to tackle?

48.	Standard I	Standard II	Standard III	Standard IV	Standard V	Standard VI
Reading	Narrative in monosyllables	One of the Narratives next in order after monosyllables in an elementary reading book used in the school	A short paragraph from an elementary reading book used in the school	A short paragraph from a more advanced reading book used in the school	A few lines of poetry from a reading book used in the first class of the school	A short ordinary paragraph in a newspaper, or other modern narrative
Writing	Form on a blackboard or slate, from dictation, letters, capital and small manuscript	Copy in manuscript character a line of print	A sentence from the same paragraph, slowly read once, and then dictated in single words	A sentence slowly dictated once by a few words at a time, from the same book, but not from the paragraph read	A sentence slowly dictated once, by a few words at a time, from a reading book used in the first class of the school	Another short ordinary paragraph in a newspaper, or other modern narrative, slowly dictated once by a few words at a time
Arithmetic	Form on a blackboard or slate, from dictation, figures up to 20; name at sight figures up to 20; add and subtract figures up to 10, orally from examples on blackboard	A sum in simple addition or subtraction, and the multiplication table	A sum in any simple rule as for a short division (inclusive)	A sum in compound rules (money)	A sum in compound rules (compound weights and measures)	A sum in practice or bills of parcels

The Revised Code of Regulations made by the Committee of the Privy Council on Education for the administration of grants to schools, 1862, quoted in J. S. Maclure, *Educational Documents, England and Wales, 1816–1963* (Chapman and Hall, 1965)

8 'A type much more common than it ought to be'

We shall now state generally the opinions we have formed respecting the course and subjects of instruction proper for these schools.

We believe that for the instruction of boys, especially when collected in a large school, it is material that there should be some one
5 principal branch of study, invested with a recognized and, if possible, a traditional importance, to which the principal weight should be assigned, and the largest share of time and attention given.

We believe that this is necessary in order to concentrate attention, to stimulate industry, to supply to the whole school a common
10 ground of literary interest and a common path of promotion.

The study of the classical languages and literature at present occupies this position in all the great English schools. It has, as we have already observed, the advantage of long possession, an advantage so great that we should certainly hesitate to advise the
15 dethronement of it, even if we were prepared to recommend a successor.

It is not, however, without reason that the foremost place has in fact been assigned to this study. Grammar is the logic of common speech, and there are few educated men who are not sensible of the
20 advantages they gained as boys from the steady practice of composition and translation, and from their introduction to etymology. The study of literature is the study, not indeed of the physical, but of the intellectual and moral worlds we live in, and of the thoughts, lives, and characters of those men whose writings or
25 whose memories succeeding generations have thought it worth while to preserve.

We are equally convinced that the best materials available to Englishmen for these studies are furnished by the languages and literature of Greece and Rome. . . .
30 Thus, when Latin was the common language of educated men, it was of primary importance to be able to speak and write Latin; so long as French is, though in a different manner and degree, a common channel of communication among educated persons in Europe, a man can hardly be called well educated who is ignorant of
35 French.

But these are difficulties which it is the business of the schoolmaster to contend with, and which careful and skilful teaching may to some extent overcome. If a youth, after four or five years spent at school, quits it at 19, unable to construe an easy bit of Latin
40 or Greek without the help of a dictionary or to write Latin grammatically, almost ignorant of geography and of the history of his own country, unacquainted with any modern language but his own, and hardly competent to write English correctly, to do a simple sum, or stumble through an easy proposition of Euclid, a

45 total stranger to the laws which govern the physical world and to its
structure, with an eye and hand unpractised in drawing and without
knowing a note of music, with an uncultivated mind and no taste for
reading or observation, his intellectual education must certainly be
accounted a failure, though there may be no fault to find with his
50 principles, character, or manners. We by no means intend to
represent this as a type of the ordinary product of English
public-school education; but speaking both from the evidence we
have received and from opportunities of observation open to all, we
must say that it is a type much more common than it ought to be,
55 making ample allowance for the difficulties before referred to, and
that the proportion of failures is therefore unduly large . . . .
  Natural science, with such slight exceptions as have been noticed
above, is practically excluded from the education of the higher
classes in England. Education with us is, in this respect, narrower
60 than it was three centuries ago, whilst science has prodigiously
extended her empire, has explored immense tracts, divided them
into provinces, introduced into them order and method, and made
them accessible to all. This exclusion is, in our view, a plain defect
and a great practical evil. It narrows unduly and injuriously the
65 mental training of the young, and the knowledge, interests, and
pursuits of men in maturer life.
       Clarendon Report on the Public Schools (1864) *Parliamentary
       Papers*, 1864, vol XX, pp 22 et seq, quoted in G. M. Young
       and W. D. Handcock, op cit

Questions

a What was the 'principal branch of study' in the public schools
   (line 5)?
b What general benefit did the study of Classics bring?
c What are the 'practice of composition and translation' and
   'etymology' (lines 20–22)? Has etymology any practical value?
d Why, according to the report, should Victorian public
   schoolboys have learned French?
e Why was the neglect of natural science 'a plain defect and a great
   practical evil' (lines 63–4)?
f Had the public schools been largely successful in educating their
   pupils according to the Commission's standards?
g For which social classes did the public schools provide an
   education?
★ h Who was Euclid?
★ i How did Thomas Arnold, Headmaster of Rugby, greatly alter
   the image of public schools?

9 'The most urgent educational need of the country'

. . . The most urgent educational need of the country is that of good schools of the third grade, that is, of those which shall carry education up to the age of 14 or 15. It is just here that the endowed schools appear most signally to fail, while nothing else takes their
5 place. The evidence is almost unanimous that just here is our most conspicuous deficiency, and that the artizans, the small shopkeepers, the smaller farmers are in many places without any convenient means of educating their children at all, and still more often have no security that what education they do get is good.
10   It is not only the case, however, that the number concerned is larger than that of any other class except the lowest, but that the wealth and prosperity of the country depend to so great a degree on the industry, and that industry on the intelligence, of those who are left thus uneducated. We have already made a special report on the
15 statements made to us regarding the inferior rate of progress said to be visible in British manufacturers, when some of the productions of this country are compared with those that were sent by other nations to the Exhibition at Paris. This is ascribed in some measure to a want of technical instruction in our artizans, as well as in their employers
20 and foremen. Such a want, however, would be a far less serious matter, if it stood alone. But we are bound to add that our evidence appears to show that our industrial classes have not even that basis of sound general education on which alone technical instruction can rest. It would not be difficult, if our artizans were otherwise well
25 educated, to establish schools for technical instruction of whatever kind might be needed. But even if such schools were generally established among us, there is reason to fear that they would fail to produce any valuable results for want of the essential material, namely, disciplined faculties and sound elementary knowledge in
30 the learners. In fact, our deficiency is not merely a deficiency in technical instruction, but, as Mr Arnold indicates, in general intelligence, and unless we remedy this want we shall gradually but surely find that our undeniable superiority in wealth and perhaps in energy will not save us from decline. If we could provide good
35 schools for our artizans up to the age of 14, then those who showed aptitude for special industrial pursuits would be in a fit condition to enter on the needed special study. But our first object should be to enable the whole of this large population, whose education we are now considering, to cultivate their children's understandings and
40 make them really intelligent men. We need schools that shall provide good instruction for the whole of the lowest portion of what is commonly called the middle class, and we cannot overstate our sense of the importance of the need. These are the schools that we have called Schools of the Third Grade . . . .

45   We have thought it our duty to inquire separately into the subject
of Girls' Schools, and we have devoted this Chapter to that branch of
the question. 'If one looks to the enormous number of unmarried
women in the middle class who have to earn their own bread, at the
great drain of the male population of this country for the army, for
50   India, and for the colonies, at the expensiveness of living here, and
consequent lateness of marriage, it seems to me that the instruction
of the girls of a middle-class family for any one who thinks much of
it, is important to the very last degree.'
       It is true that this conviction, as relating to the Middle Classes,
55   may be looked on as recent and still growing, and as one which still
greatly needs to be inculcated on and accepted by parents of that
class. We have had much evidence showing the general indifference
of parents to girls' education, both in itself and as compared to that of
boys. It leads to a less immediate and tangible pecuniary result; there
60   is a long-established and inveterate prejudice, though it may not
often be distinctly expressed, that girls are less capable of mental
cultivation, and less in need of it, than boys.
            Taunton   Report   on   endowed   schools   1867–1868,
       Parliamentary Papers, 1867–1868, vol XXVIII, pp 78–88,
       546–661, quoted in G. M. Young and W. D. Handcock, op
       cit

Questions

a   What were artizans (line 6)?
b   What social class did 'the artizans, the small shopkeepers and the
    smaller farmers' (lines 6–7) constitute?
ι   What kind of education was thought suitable for this class?
★ d   How did their technical instruction differ from the study of
    natural science in the public schools?
e   Why was it not possible to provide a good technical education
    without a sound general education?
f   What views did the Commission hold on intelligence?
g   Why had girls' education been neglected?
h   Why was a major change in girls' education needed?
★ i   Explain the social thinking behind the Clarendon and Taunton
    Reports (extracts 8 and 9).

10   'Our object is . . . to fill up gaps'

Now, what are the results (of the nation's educational provision so
far)? They are what we might have expected; much imperfect
education and much absolute ignorance . . . . We find a vast
number of children badly taught or utterly untaught, because there
5   are too few schools and too many bad schools . . . . Our object is to

complete the present voluntary system, to fill up gaps, sparing the
public money where it can be done without, procuring the assistance
. . . of parents, and welcoming . . . the aid of . . . benevolent
gentlemen.
10   . . . the main principles . . . for securing efficient school provision
. . . are two in number. Legal enactment, that there shall be efficient
schools everywhere throughout the kingdom. Compulsory
provision of such schools if and where needed . . . .
        I believe it is not in the power of any central department to
15   undertake such a duty (of providing the money). Consider also the
enormous power it would give the central administration . . . .
Therefore, where we have proved the educational need we supply it
by local administration – that is, by means of rates aided by money
voted by Parliament, expended under local management, with
20   central inspection and control.
        I have said that there will be compulsory provision . . . . How do
we propose to apply it? By school boards elected by the district.
        The school boards are to provide the education. Who are to pay
for it? In the first place, shall we give up the school fees . . . ? I at
25   once say the Government are not prepared to do it. Nevertheless . . .
we give the school boards power to establish special free schools
(and) to give free tickets to parents who think they really cannot
afford to pay . . . (without) any stigma of pauperism.
        . . . Compulsory attendance . . . from five to twelve. What is the
30   purpose of this Bill? Briefly this, to bring elementary education
within the reach of every English home, aye, and within the reach of
those children who have no home.
        W. E. Forster on the Education Bill, 17 February 1870,
        Hansard, 3rd series, CXCIX, 440–66, quoted in J. S.
        Maclure, op cit

Questions

a   What were the principles included in the Bill which were
    designed to secure 'efficient school provision' (line 10)?
b   In what ways does this Bill show a change in attitude within
    parliament?
c   Why did the Bill set up a local administration for the provision of
    education?
d   What was the local education authority set up by the Bill?
e   What powers over the local school and over the local education
    authorities were kept by central government?
★ f   Why was Forster concerned that the provision of 'free tickets'
    should not convey 'any stigma of pauperism' (lines 27–8)? Is it
    likely that they were seen to be in fact such a stigma?

11 'More general diffusion of technical education'

. . . Not so many years have passed since the time when it would still have been a matter for argument whether, in order to maintain the high position which this country has attained in the industrial arts, it is incumbent upon us to take care that our managers, our foremen,
5 and our workmen, should, in the degrees compatible with their circumstances, combine theoretical instruction with their acknowledged practical skill. No argument of this kind is needed at the present day. In nearly all the great industrial centres – in the metropolis, in Glasgow, in Manchester, Liverpool, Oldham, Leeds,
10 Bradford, Huddersfield, Keighley, Sheffield, Nottingham, Birmingham, the Potteries, and elsewhere – more or less flourishing schools of science and art of various grades, together with numerous art and science classes exist and their influence may be traced in the production of the localities in which they are placed. The schools
15 established by Sir W. Armstrong at Elswick; by the London and North-Western Railway Company at Crewe; and those of Messrs Mather and Platt of Salford, in connection with their engineering works, testify to the importance attached by employers to the theoretical training of young mechanics. The efforts of Messrs
20 Denny, the eminent shipbuilders of Dumbarton, for encouraging the instruction of their apprentices and for rewarding their workmen for meritorious improvements in details applicable to their work, are proofs of this appreciation. The evidence of Mr Richardson of Oldham, and of Mr Mather of Salford, is emphatic as to their
25 experience of its economical value.

Without more particularly referring to the valuable work in the past, accomplished by the numerous mechanics' institutes spread over the country, many of them of long standing, we may point out that they are now largely remodelling their constitutions in order to
30 bring up their teaching to the level of modern requirements, as regards technical instruction. The example of the Manchester Mechanics' Institute may be studied in this connection . . . .

Natural science is finding its way surely, though slowly, into the curriculum of our older English universities, and of our secondary
35 schools. It is becoming a prominent feature in the upper divisions of the elementary board schools in our large towns. There are scarcely any important metallurgical works in the kingdom without a chemical laboratory in which the raw materials and products are daily subjected to careful analysis by trained chemists. The
40 attainments of the young men who have been trained in the Royal Naval College at Greenwich recommend them for remunerative employment by our great shipbuilding firms . . . .

Thus, there is no necessity to 'preach to the converted', and we may confine ourselves to such considerations as bear upon the

45   improvement and more general diffusion of technical education at
      home, in accordance with the conditions and needs of our industrial
      population.
            Royal Commission on Technical Instruction, 1884,
            Parliamentary Papers, 1884, vol XXIX (c.3981), pp 513–14,
            quoted in W. D. Handcock, *EHD*, vol XII(2) (Unwin,
            1956)

Questions

a   What 'matter for argument' (line 2) had recently been settled in the
    provision of technical education?
b   What kind of education was available in technical subjects?
c   Who frequently pioneered technical education?
d   By what means was greater theoretical understanding being
    brought into technical education and into education generally?
e   What were the likely limitations, if any, of the types of education
    outlined above?

12   'One authority for education'

Our reform . . . must, in the first place, establish one authority for
education – technical, secondary, primary – possessed of powers
which may enable it to provide for the adequate training of teachers,
and for welding higher technical and higher secondary education
5   onto the university system. In the second place, I conclude that this
one authority for education, being, as it is, responsible for a heavy
cost to the ratepayers, should be the rating authority of the district.
In the third place, I lay down that the voluntary schools must be
placed in a position in which they can worthily play their necessary
10   and inevitable part in the scheme of national education.
    . . . Our education authority is the County Council in counties
and the Borough Council in county boroughs. They will work
through a committee . . . a majority of members appointed by the
Council . . . another portion . . . will consist of persons experienced
15   in education. The Councils of Boroughs of over 10,000 and of urban
districts of over 20,000 . . . may become the absolute authority as
regards primary education. They retain their existing powers as to
technical education and they also become the authority for
secondary education concurrently with the County Councils.
20   Whether (public elementary) schools are voluntary or rate-erected
. . . the local education authority . . . will be absolute master of the
whole scheme of secular education in every elementary school in its
district.
    We propose that on the county or borough rate shall be thrown
25   the whole cost of maintaining every school under the local
authority . . . . The managers of the voluntary schools will be

required . . . to keep (their schools) in good repair, and to make all reasonable . . . improvements.

Speech of Rt. Hon. A. J. Balfour on the Introduction of the Education Bill, 24 March 1902

Questions

a Why was the 'rating authority of the district' (line 7) made the local education authority?

b What were the responsibilities of county council and county borough education committees?

c How did Balfour try to ensure that educational ideas should influence the deliberations of the local education authorities?

d How independent were the voluntary schools after the passage of the Act?

e What were the responsibilities of local voluntary schools' managers to be in the future?

f Was Britain now provided with an integrated educational system?

13 'A larger and more enlightened freedom'

Firstly, we desire to improve the administrative organisation of education. Secondly, we are anxious to secure for every boy and girl in this country an elementary school life up to the age of fourteen which shall be unimpeded by the competing claims of industry.
5 Thirdly, we desire to establish part-time day continuation schools which every young person in the country shall be compelled to attend unless he or she is undergoing some suitable form of alternative instruction. Fourthly, we make a series of proposals for the development of the higher forms of elementary education and
10 for the improvement of the physical condition of the children and young persons under instruction. Fifthly, we desire to consolidate the elementary school Grants and, sixthly, we wish to make an effective survey of the whole educational provision of the country and to bring private educational institutions into closer and more
15 convenient relations to the national system.

I now come to the most novel . . . provision in the Bill. We propose that . . . every young person no longer under any obligation to attend a public elementary school shall attend (a) continuation school . . . for a period of 320 hours in the year, or . . .
20 eight hours a week for forty weeks . . . young persons will be liberated from industrial toil for the equivalent of three half days a week during forty weeks – two half-days to be spent in school, while one will be a half-holiday.

. . . We argue that (this) compulsion . . . will be . . . an essential

25   condition of a larger and more enlightened freedom, which will tend
to stimulate the civic spirit, to promote general culture and technical
knowledge and to diffuse a steadier judgment and a better informed
opinion through the whole body of the community.

H. A. L. Fisher introducing the Education Bill, Hansard, 10
August 1917, quoted in J. S. Maclure, op cit

Questions

a   What is meant by a school life 'unimpeded by the competing
claims of industry' (line 4)?
b   What benefit were the continuation schools expected to bring?
★   c   Why did Fisher want to bring private educational institutions
'into closer . . . relations to the national system' (lines 14–15)?
d   How did Fisher think the nation would benefit from an improved
system of education?
★   e   Why did the continuation schools not develop?

14   The Modern School

We recommend that . . . an additional year should be added to the
general school life, and the leaving age should be raised to fifteen.

The scheme which we advocate can be simply stated. It is that . . .
all the children of the country . . . after spending the first years of
5   school life in a primary school should spend the last three or four
years in a well-equipped and well-staffed modern school . . . under
the stimulus of practical work and realistic studies . . . .

It is desirable that education up to 11+ should be known by the
general name of Primary Education, and education after 11 by the
10   general name of Secondary Education, and that the schools . . .
which are concerned with the secondary stage of education should be
called by the following designations:-

(i) Schools of a 'Secondary' type . . . which at present pursue . . . a
predominantly literary or scientific curriculum, to be known as
15   Grammar Schools.

(ii) Schools of the type of the existing Selective Central Schools
. . . to be known as Modern Schools.

(iii) Schools of the type of the present Non-selective Central
Schools . . . also to be known as Modern Schools . . . .

20   *Curriculum*
The general characteristics of Modern Schools will be as follows:-

1. . . . courses will . . . be simpler and more limited in scope than
those in Grammar Schools.

2. . . . more time will be devoted to handwork and similar
25   pursuits.

3. . . . . the treatment of the subject . . . should be practical in the broadest sense and brought directly into relation with the facts of everyday life.

The Hadow Report, 1926, quoted in J. S. Maclure, op cit

Questions

★   a   Why was the leaving age not raised to fifteen before 1939?

    b   At what age did children move from primary to secondary schooling? Was the age well chosen?

    c   What types of post primary education were now to be available up to the age of 15?

    d   In what ways was the curriculum of the Modern School to be different from the Grammar Schools?

    e   What is meant by 'practical work and realistic studies' (line 7)?

    f   What criticism could be levelled at the Modern Schools once they were given a curriculum more 'limited in scope' (line 22) than the Grammar Schools?

    g   What did the Modern Schools really need in order to gain widespread acceptance?

★   h   How much do you think social values underlying educational provision changed between 1830 and 1926?

VIII   Poor Law to Insurance

Introduction

The Poor Law Amendment Act, 1834, was designed to provide help only for the destitute. Every disincentive was put before the able-bodied poor to prevent applications for relief by imposing a test: the workhouse. Only those desperate for help would seek it in the institutions to be developed by unions of parishes, with their own salaried officials, directed by boards of guardians, supervised by the central body of Poor Law Commissioners.

Workhouse material provision was good: the Commissions proved model building designs and a variety of diets. Under normal circumstances inmates could not suffer from lack of shelter or shortage of food. But the harshness of the system was to be found in its discipline and routine, its calculation to destroy the dignity of the individual and above all the segregation of its inmates. The ultimate result of the workhouse system was 'a deep alienation of the population from the machinery of official relief' (G. M. Young and W. D. Handcock, *English Historical Documents*, XII(1), p 690).

Although most of the country was provided with Union Workhouses before 1850, outdoor relief payments continued to be made in some parts of the country. Local factors, the character of the administration, the degree of protest expressed and above all the nature of the economy were deciding factors. Where whole communities were employed in the same trade or industry, industrial depression could create problems with which the law could not cope. Parts of Lancashire and Yorkshire were not organised in the new way until the 1860s.

Problems raised by the laws of settlement, based on parentage, birth and, for women, marriage were alleviated by the Union Chargeability Act, 1865, which spread burdens of the rates over the whole union instead of upon parishes. The Poor Law Commissioners, to help overpopulated areas, encouraged migration schemes both within the country and abroad to the British colonies.

From 1870 onwards the more rigorous application of the law brought much harsher treatment for the 'undeserving poor', particularly vagrants. At the same time it was beginning to be realised that all the categories of the poor were not best treated in one institution. Moves were made to put children into homes and integrate their education with the Elementary Schools. Standards of medical care were improved and the aged, a focus of deep public concern, were to be provided in future with Old Age Pensions (1908).

The investigations of people like Charles Booth in London supplemented public enquiries to demonstrate that the real causes of poverty were not moral, but unemployment and low wages. The new attitude generated many changes: Unemployed Workmen Act, 1905, Trade Boards Act and setting up of Labour Exchanges, 1909, the National Insurance Act, 1911. Nonetheless the moral assertions of the Poor Law were slow in dying. Not until 1948 could it be confidently said: 'At last we have buried the poor law'.

1 Principles of the New System

(a) We are induced to believe that a compulsory provision for the relief of the indigent can be generally administered on a sound and well-defined principle; and that under the operation of this principle, the assurance that no-one need perish may be rendered more
5 complete than at present.

The first and most essential of all conditions (is) . . . that his (i.e. the pauper's) situation on the whole shall not be made as eligible as the situation of the independent labourer of the lowest class. Throughout the evidence it is shown, that in proportion as the
10 condition of any pauper class is elevated above the condition of independent labourers, the condition of the independent class is depressed; their industry is impaired, the employment becomes unsteady, and its remuneration in wages is reduced. Such persons, therefore, are under the strongest inducements to quit the less
15 eligible class of labourers, and enter the more eligible class of paupers. The converse is the effect when the pauper class is placed in its proper position, below the condition of the independent labourer.

> Report from His Majesty's Commissioners for inquiring into the Administration and Practical Operation of the Poor Laws (1834), pp 227–8, quoted in G. M. Young and W. D. Handcock, op cit

(b) 2. The practice of making allowances of clothing to the children of able-bodied labourers going into service appears to prevail in
20 many unions.

It is manifest that the practice of making allowances of clothing to the children of labourers going into service cannot increase the total amount of employment; that every person who obtains employment on account of the allowance of clothes from the parish,

25 must prevent another person who has not that advantage from obtaining employment; and, consequently, that such allowances are detrimental to the independent labourer.

> Instructions of the Poor Laws Commissioners, *Parliamentary Papers* 1846, vol V (i), p 93, quoted in G. M. Young and W. D. Handcock, op cit

Questions

a What is the minimum the Act is prepared to provide for the poor?

★ b What evidence from the operation of the old Poor Law could have been used to suggest that poor relief payments had caused wages to fall?

c How do the principles expressed here agree with the ideas of the political economists and Malthus?

d What does 'less eligible' (lines 14–15) mean?

e What do you think were the main purposes of the Poor Law Amendment Act?

f What would appear to be the great disadvantage suffered by the workhouse inmate from less eligibility in situations such as that in extract b?

2 Disorderly and Refractory

Any pauper who shall neglect to observe such of the regulations herein contained as are applicable to and binding on him:-

Or who shall make any noise when silence is ordered to be kept;

Or shall use obscene or profane language;

5   Or shall by word or deed insult or revile any person;

Or shall threaten to strike or to assault any person;

Or shall not duly cleanse his person;

Or shall refuse or neglect to work, after having been required to do so;

10   Or shall pretend sickness;

Or shall play at cards or other games of chance;

Or shall enter or attempt to enter, without permission, the ward or yard appropriated to any class of paupers other than that to which he belongs;

15   Or shall misbehave in going to, at, or returning from public worship out of the workhouse, or at prayers in the workhouse;

Or shall return after the appointed time of absence, when allowed to quit the workhouse temporarily;

Or shall wilfully disobey any lawful order of any officer of the

20   workhouse;

Shall be deemed DISORDERLY.

Any pauper who shall, within seven days, repeat any one or commit more than one of the offences specified in Article 34;

25 Or who shall by word or deed insult or revile the master or matron, or any other officer of the workhouse, or any of the Guardians;

Or shall wilfully disobey any lawful order of the master or matron after such order shall have been repeated;

Or shall unlawfully strike or otherwise unlawfully assault any
30 person;

Or shall wilfully or mischievously damage or soil any property whatsoever belonging to the Guardians;

Or shall wilfully waste or spoil any provisions, stock, tools, or materials for work, belonging to the Guardians;
35 Or shall be drunk;

Or shall commit any act of indecency;

Or shall wilfully disturb the other inmates during prayers or divine worship;

Shall be deemed REFRACTORY.

40 It shall be lawful for the master of the workhouse, with or without the direction of the Board of Guardians, to punish any disorderly pauper by substituting, during a time not greater than forty-eight hours, for his or her dinner, as prescribed by the dietary, a meal consisting of eight ounces of bread, or one pound of cooked
45 potatoes, and also by withholding from him during the same period, all butter, cheese, tea, sugar, or broth, which such pauper would otherwise receive, at any meal during the time aforesaid.

And it shall be lawful for the Board of Guardians, by a special direction to be entered on their minutes, to order any refractory
50 pauper to be punished by confinement in a separate room, with or without an alteration of diet, similar in kind and duration to that prescribed in Art. 36 for disorderly paupers.
        Parliamentary Papers, 1842, vol XIX, p 42–3

Questions

a What impression of workhouse organisation do you obtain from this code of discipline?
b What effect do you think these regulations were designed to have upon the inmates?
c Do you think the master of the workhouse was given adequate authority? Could that authority be abused?
d Do you think that the inmates found it easy to obey the regulations?

3 Dietary for Able-bodied Paupers

| | | Breakfast | | Dinner | | | | | Supper | |
		Bread oz	Gruel pints	Cooked Meat oz	Potatoes or other Vegs lb	Soup pints	Bread oz	Cheese oz	Bread oz	Cheese oz
Sunday	Men	8	1½				7	2	6	1½
	Women	6	1½				6	1½	5	1½
Monday	Men	8	1½				7	2	6	1½
	Women	6	1½				6	1½	5	1½
Tuesday	Men	8	1½	8	¾				6	1½
	Women	6	1½	6	¾				5	1½
Wednesday	Men	8	1½				7	2	6	1½
	Women	6	1½				6	1½	5	1½
Thursday	Men	8	1½			1½	6		6	1½
	Women	6	1½			1½	5		6	1½
Friday	Men	8	1½				7	2	6	1½
	Women	6	1½				6	1½	5	1½
Saturday	Men	8	1½	Bacon 5	¾				6	1½
	Women	6	1½	4	¾				5	1½

20 Old people of 60 years of age and upwards may be allowed one
ounce of tea, five ounces of butter, and seven ounces of sugar per
week, in lieu of gruel for breakfast, if deemed expedient. Children
under nine years of age to be directed at discretion; above nine, to be
allowed the same quantities as women. Sick to be dieted as directed
25 by the medical officer.

Parliamentary Papers, 1836, vol XXIX (1), p 57

Questions

a Do you think this is a better diet than that which could be
afforded by agricultural labourers paid between 9s. and 12s. per
week?

b What comment should be made on the diet for children?

c Why do you think that additional items were suggested by the
Commissions for the aged poor?

4 The Andover Workhouse Scandal

25. That in the month of February 1836 several forms of dietary
were set down by the Poor Law Commissioners, of which one,
marked No. 3, was selected by the Board of Guardians for adoption
in the workhouse, and sanctioned by the Commissioners.

Report, *Parliamentary Papers*, 1846, V(i), p XIX

5 Evidence of Charles Lewis, labourer.
9828 (Mr Wakley) What work were you employed about when you
were in the workhouse? –
I was employed breaking bones.
9829 Were other men engaged in the same work? –
10 Yes.
9830 Was that the only employment you had? –
That was the only employment I had at the time I was there.
9831 Was the smell very bad? –
Very bad.
15 9832 Did it appear to affect your health? –
It did a great deal mine, and appeared to affect the others.
9833 How many men were so employed? –
Whether it was nine or ten boxes round the room, I don't
recollect.
20 9834 Was it a close room or shed? –
It was a very close room.
9835 How did you break them? –
We had a large iron bar to break them with.
9836 Something like a rammer? –
25 Yes.

9837 Had you no other employment at all? –
No, not while I was there, but breaking the bones.
9838 What sort of bones did they appear to be? –
All sorts.
30 9839 During the time you were so employed, did you ever see any
of the men gnaw anything or eat anything from those
bones? –
I have seen them eat marrow out of the bones.
9840 You were not examined before Mr Parker, the Assistant
35 Commissioner? –
No.
9841 Have you often seen them eat the marrow? –
I have.
9842 Did they state why they did it? –
40 I really believe they were very hungry.
9843 Did you yourself feel extremely hungry at that time? –
I did, but my stomach would not take it.
9844 You could not swallow the marrow? –
No.
45 9845 Did you see any of the men gnaw the meat from the bones? –
Yes.
9846 Did they use to steal the bones and hide them away? –
Yes.
9847 Have you seen them have a scramble and quarrel amongst the
50 bones? –
I do not know that I have seen them scramble, but I have seen
them hide them.
9848 And when a fresh set of bones came in, did they keep a sharp
look-out for the best? –
55 Yes.
9849 Was that a regular thing? –
While I was there.
9853 Was that rammer composed entirely of iron? –
Yes.
60 9854 And what do you suppose the weight of the iron was? –
I should say 20 lbs or 25 lbs.
9855 Had it any affect on your hands? –
Yes; my hands were blistered very much the time I were at it.
Minutes of evidence, *Parliamentary Papers*, 1846, vol V(1),
pp 382–3

Questions

a Do you consider the hunger of the inmates was caused by the
dietary adapted by the Andover union? If not, what other
possible reasons could be examined?
b Why was the smell from the bones so bad? Was the workhouse

following the Commissioners' recommendation to use only dry bones?

c Was this work arduous for the workhouse inmates?

d Of what use were crushed bones? Could the product benefit the workhouse?

5 Segregation in Workhouses

Even in the larger workhouses internal subdivisions do not afford the means of classification, where the inmates dine in the same rooms, or meet or see each other in the ordinary business of the place. . . . Much, however, has been accomplished . . . but much
5 more . . . may be effected, and at a less expense by the measures that we proceed to suggest.

At least four classes are necessary:- 1. The aged and really impotent; 2. the children; 3. the able-bodied females; 4. the able-bodied males . . . . It appears to us that both the requisite
10 classification and the requisite superintendence may be better obtained in separate buildings than under a single roof. If effected in the latter mode, large buildings must be erected, since few of the existing buildings are of the requisite size . . . .

Although such is the general tenor of the evidence, we cannot state
15 there may not be some districts where new workhouses would be found requisite, but we have no doubt . . . the erection of the appropriate offices, though apparently expensive, would ultimately be found economical . . . . Considerable economy would also be practicable in combined workhouses, by varying the nature of the
20 supplies . . . .

To effect these purposes we recommend that the Central Board be empowered to cause any number of parishes that they may think convenient to be incorporated for the purpose of workhouse management, and for providing new workhouses.

Poor Law Report, 1834, pp 306–14, quoted in G. M. Young and W. D. Handcock, op cit

Questions

a What was the main concern of the Commissioners when giving consideration to workhouse accommodation?

b Why were people classified?

c When could families meet?

d How do you think the poor responded to segregation in workhouses?

e What recommendation did the Commissioners make to enable parishes to provide workhouses for their poor?

6 A Workhouse near Manchester

The building is huge, perfectly clean, and well maintained: big
courtyards, gardens round the building, a view of fields and tall
trees, chapel, public rooms twenty feet high. It looks as if the
founders and administrators of the place have taken pride in doing a
5   handsome and useful job.

There was no bad smell anywhere about the place. The beds were
almost white and provided with patterned bed-spreads. The oldest
and most infirm women had white bonnets and new clothes . . . .

The kitchen is enormous: a structure of masonry contains eight or
10   ten boilers in which oatmeal gruel is cooked: this is the principal
article of their diet. Each inmate receives two pounds of 'oat-meal' a
day, a pound and a half of potatoes, half a pound of bread and, four
times a week, four ounces of minced-meat or boned meat. The only
drink is water, excepting in case of sickness.

15   We were considerably surprised: beside the rows of hovels in
which the poor live, this place is a palace. One of us gravely
requested our friend and escort to keep a place for him in the
institution where he could spend his old age. Consider this: a
labourer at Manchester or Liverpool can barely afford to eat meat
20   once a week, yet has to work ten hours a day! Here, a person in good
health works six hours a day, has newspapers and the Bible to read,
as well as a few other good books and Reviews; and he can live in
pure air and see trees. Yet at the time of writing there is not one
able-bodied person to be found in a workhouse: the one we saw is
25   almost empty and will only be filled when winter comes . . . .

What is the reason for this repugnance? I saw, today, an old
woman sorting through a heap of rubbish, and picking out remnants
of vegetables with her thin hands: she may have been one of those
who are unwilling to give up their drop of gin. But what of the
30   others? I am told that they will stick to their 'home' and their liberty
at any price and cannot bear to be shut up and become subject to
discipline. 'They prefer to be free and to starve.'

But then, the children? All those little ones, with their white skulls
showing through the tow-coloured hair, crammed into a single
35   room with their thin and haggard mothers – how can the fathers bear
such a sight? They do bear it, they do not want to be parted from
them . . . .

The workhouse is looked upon as a prison and the poor make it a
point of honour never to enter one.

> Hippolyte Taine, *Notes on England*, trans. E. Hyams (Thames
> and Hudson, 1957), pp 237–8

Questions

a   Were the inmates made to work hard?

b   What leisure facilities did they have? Was boredom possible?
c   What did the 'almost white' of the beds, the 'patterned bed-spreads', the 'white bonnets' and 'new clothes' reveal and, at the same time, hide (lines 7–8)?
d   Would one of Taine's friends really have wanted to spend his old age there?
e   Why did the poor determine 'never to enter one' (line 39)?
f   Were there other forms of assistance for which the poor could apply?

7   The Removal of Paupers

Poor Law Board, Whitehall, S.W.,
6th April 1866.

Sir,

5   I am directed by the Poor Law Board to communicate again with the Guardians on the subject of that part of the Union Chargeability Act of 1865 which relates to the removal of paupers.

That Act having put an end to Parochial Chargeability in the Union has transferred the power of obtaining orders of removal to the Board of Guardians.

10   They strongly recommend to Boards of Guardians the exercise, as far as practicable, of a spirit of mutual forbearance in regard to the removal of paupers who may be removable.

They deem it advisable to recall to the attention of the Guardians a consideration of the limits which have been imposed upon their

15   power in this matter by the Legislature.

No person who has resided for one whole year in the Union, whether in one or in several parts of it, without interruption and without relief, can be removed from it. Periods of relief do not operate as an interruption of the residence, but are only not to be

20   calculated as part of the time of residence.

Moreover, periods of residence, under certain specific circumstances, both in and out of the Union, are prevented from being computed in the calculation of the time of residence, or from operating as an interruption of the residence.

25   No widow residing with her husband at the time of his death can be removed within the first year of her widowhood.

Deserted wives also, after a residence of one year from the time of their desertion, without relief, are exempt from removal.

Children cannot be removed from their parents or some other

30   relatives with whom they may be residing, and orphans derive from their parents the exemption which the latter had acquired at their death.

Poor Law Board's explanation of the Union Chargeability Act, 1865, *Parliamentary Papers*, 1866, vol XXXV, pp 28–9, quoted in G. M. Young and W. D. Handcock, op cit

Questions

a Why had parishes sought to remove people needing relief? Where had such people been sent?

b How did the Act limit the powers of removal?

c Why did the Poor Law Board recommend a 'spirit of mutual forbearance' (line 11)?

★ d Why was this change in the laws of settlement valuable to workers in the new industrial towns?

8 No change needed . . . ?

(a)23. The particulars as to the proportion of aged persons relieved during a year for several counties are examined by Sir Hugh Owen, and the figures are unquestionably, as he says, in many respects 'very startling'. The fact that 35 per cent of the population of
5 London over sixty-five are returned as receiving relief other than medical relief, and that 23 (per cent) of this 35 per cent receive it in poor law establishments, is especially remarkable.

24. but in reviewing the figures and drawing conclusions from them several facts must be borne in mind. The number of persons
10 receiving relief at some time in the course of a year does not by any means represent the number who are continuously destitute. Relief is in many cases only sought at intervals to tide over sickness and other special emergencies. This is illustrated by the results which Mr Booth has given us for Paddington, where it is found that the aged
15 recipients of indoor relief in a year exceed by 50 per cent the recipients in one day; but if two years are taken the one day figure is nearly doubled. The figures he gives show that, at all ages, occasional recourse is had to the poor law by those who do not permanently rely on it, and that such persons to a large extent keep
20 entirely off the rates for long periods. We think it right, however, to point out that an aged person above sixty-five, who comes only at long intervals for relief, may often be a person who is generally averse to such assistance, and only accepts it under pressure of illness or severe distress. The ordinary condition of such persons must be
25 only just removed from pauperism and calls for sympathy and consideration. There are also many aged poor who are destitute so far as their own resources are concerned, but who are kept off the rates by the assistance of friends and by private charity. Such persons must sometimes endure great privation in their effort to avoid
30 application for official relief, and they form a class quite as deserving of consideration.

Summary . . .

2. We are of opinion that no fundamental alterations are needed in the existing system of poor relief as it affects the aged. At the same

35　time we are convinced that there is a strong feeling that in the
administration of relief there should be greater discrimination
between the respectable aged who become destitute and those whose
destitution is distinctly the consequence of their own misconduct.
Report of the Royal Commission on the Aged Poor,
Parliamentary Papers, 1895, vol XIV, pp 20–28, quoted in
W. D. Handcock, op cit

(b) It is not in the name of the people but to the people, that I would
40　speak, in advocating the endowment of old age as at once a practical
and possible means of giving a surer footing to those who now,
trying to stand, too often fall and sometimes sink altogether. I
advocate it as bringing with it something of that security necessary
to a higher standard of life. A security of position which will
45　stimulate rather than weaken the play of individuality on which
progress and prosperity depend.
Charles Booth, *Pauperism and the Endowment of Old Age*
(1982), p 241, quoted in W. D. Handcock, op cit

Questions

a　What statistics were 'very startling' and 'especially remarkable'
(lines 4 and 7)? Why were they so?
b　How does the Report consider these statistics ought to be
interpreted?
c　What people were worthy of 'sympathy and consideration' (lines
25–6)? Was this sympathy to be given practical form?
d　What criterion does the Board suggest ought to be imposed in
deciding who should receive relief?
e　What was the outlook for those destitute through their own
misconduct?
f　In what way did Charles Booth think old age pensions would
give a 'surer footing' (line 41)?
g　Would pensions encourage a 'higher standard of life' (line 44) for
the aged?
h　How could 'the play of individuality' stimulate 'progress and
prosperity' (lines 45–6)?

9　Old Age Pensions

1.(1) Every person in whose case the conditions laid down by this
Act for the receipt of an old age pension . . . are fulfilled, shall be
entitled to receive such a pension . . . .

(2) An old age pension under this Act shall be at the rate set forth
5　in the schedule to this Act.

(3) The sums required for the payment of old age pensions under
this Act shall be paid out of moneys provided by parliament.

(4) The receipt of an old age pension under this Act shall not deprive the pensioner of any franchise, right, or privilege, or subject him to any disability.

2. The statutory conditions for the receipt of an old age pension by any person are,

(1) The person must have attained the age of seventy.

(2) The person must satisfy the pension authorities that for at least twenty years . . . he has been a British subject.

(3) The person must satisfy the pension authorities that his yearly means as calculated under this Act do not exceed thirty-one pounds ten shillings.

4. (1) In calculating the means of a person for the purpose of this Act account shall be taken of . . . the income which that person may reasonably expect to receive during the succeeding year.

Schedule

Means of Pensioner	*Rate of pension per week* *s d*
Where the yearly means of the pensioner as calculated under this Act do not exceed 21l.	5 0
exceed 21l. but do not exceed 23l. 12s. 6d	4 0
exceed 23l. 12s. 6d, but do not exceed 26l. 5s	3 0
exceed 26l. 5s, but do not exceed 28l. 17s. 6d	2 0
exceed 28l. 17s. 6d, but do not exceed 31l. 10s.	1 0
Exceed 31l. 10s.	No pension

Old Age Pensions Act, 1908, 8 Edw 7. c. 40, quoted in W. D. Handcock, op cit

Questions

a List all the qualifications necessary for receipt of a pension.
b What justification can be made for setting the pensionable age at 70?
★ *c* Why did parliament in 1908 directly contradict the Report of the Royal Commission for the Aged Poor produced thirteen years earlier?
d What category of person mentioned in Chapter 3 would be excluded from receiving an old age pension?

10 Labour Exchanges and some Unemployment Insurance

Yes, but the House may say what is the connection of all this with

Labour Exchanges. I must apologise for detaining the House so
long –
    Mr John Ward: This is the most interesting part of your speech.
5   Mr Churchill: But the machinery of the insurance office has been
gone into with great detail, and we propose as at present advised to
follow the German example of insurance cards or books, to which
stamps will be affixed every week. For as soon as a man in an insured
trade is without employment, if he has kept to the rules of the
10 system, all he will have to do is to take his card to the nearest Labour
Exchange, which will be responsible, in conjunction with the
insurance office, either for finding him a job or for paying him his
benefits. I am very glad, indeed, to have availed myself of the
opportunity which my right hon. friend has given me to submit this
15 not inconsiderable proposal in general outline, so that the bill for
Labour Exchanges which I will introduce tomorrow may not be
misjudged as if it stood by itself, and was not part of a considered,
coordinated, and connected scheme to grasp with this hideous
crushing evil which has oppressed for so long the mind of every one
20 who cares about social reform. We cannot deal with the insurance
policy this session for five reasons.
    We have not the time now. We have not got the money yet. The
finances of this insurance scheme have got to be adjusted and
interwoven with the finances of the other schemes which my right
25 hon. friend the Chancellor of the Exchequer is engaged upon now for
dealing with various forms of invalidity and other insurance. In the
next place, Labour Exchanges are the necessary preliminary. We
have got to get the apparatus of the Labour Exchanges into working
order before this system of insurance can effectually be established or
30 worked.
    Winston S. Churchill, 19 May 1907, Hansard, 5th Series,
    507 ff, quoted in W. D. Handcock, op cit

Questions

a Why was the setting-up of labour exchanges a 'necessary
    preliminary' (line 27) to a scheme of national insurance?
b What responsibility did Churchill place upon the labour
    exchanges?
c How do you think the 'German example of insurance cards' (line
    7) was intended to work?
★ d Was such an insurance scheme likely to be expensive?
★ e Who was Chancellor of the Exchequer? What difficulties did he
    find in making the necessary funds available?

11 Distress Committees and Relief Work

1.(1) For the purposes of this Act there shall be established, by order
of the Local Government Board under this Act, a distress committee

of the council of every metropolitan borough in London, consisting
partly of members of the borough council and partly of members of
5   the board of guardians of every poor law union wholly or partly
within the borough and of persons experienced in the relief of
distress, and a central body for the whole of the administrative
county of London, consisting partly of members of, and selected by,
the distress committees and of members of, and selected by, the
10 London County Council, and partly of persons co-opted to be
additional members of the body, and partly, if the order so provides,
of persons nominated by the Local Government Board.

(2) The distress committee shall make themselves acquainted
with the conditions of labour within their area, and when so required
15 by the central body shall receive, inquire into and discriminate
between   any   applications   made   to   them   from   persons
unemployed . . . .

(3) If the distress committee are satisfied that any such applicant is
honestly desirous of obtaining work, but is temporarily unable to do
20 so . . . they may endeavour to obtain work for the applicant, or, if
they think the case is one for treatment by the central body rather
than by themselves, refer the case to the central body . . . .

(4) The central body shall superintend and, as far as possible,
coordinate the action of the distress committees, and aid the efforts
25 of those committees by establishing, taking over, or assisting labour
exchanges and employment registers, and by the collection of
information and otherwise as they think fit.

(5) The central committee may, if they think fit, in any case of an
unemployed person referred to them by a distress committee, assist
30 that person by aiding the emigration or removal to another area of that
person and any of his dependents, or by providing, or contributing
towards the provision of, temporary work . . . .

2.(1) There shall be established by order of the Local Government
Board for each municipal borough and urban district . . . a distress
35 committee of the council for the purposes of this Act.

The Unemployed Workmen Act, 1905, quoted in W. D.
Handcock, op cit

Questions

a   What category of person was the Act designed to help?
b   What kinds of people would be coopted because they were
'experienced in the relief of distress' (lines 6–7)? Where would
they have gained their experience?
c   What improvements in the administration of relief was the Act
trying to produce?
d   For what period of time was work to be provided?
e   How would the unemployed respond to Clause 5? What
problems would such removal cause?

12　A System of National Insurance

Now comes the question, which leads up to the decision of the Government to take action. What is the explanation that only a portion of the working-classes have made provision against sickness and against unemployment? Is it they consider it not necessary?
5　Quite the reverse, as I shall prove by figures. In fact, those who stand most in need of it make up the bulk of the uninsured. Why? Because very few can afford to pay the premiums, and pay them continuously, which enable a man to provide against those three contingencies. As a matter of fact, you could not provide against all
10　those three contingencies anything which would be worth a workman's while, without paying at any rate 1s.6d. or 2s. per week at the very lowest. There are a multitude of the working classes who cannot spare that, and ought not to be asked to spare it, because it involves the deprivation of children of the necessaries of life.
15　Therefore they are compelled to elect, and the vast majority choose to insure against death alone. Those who can afford to take up two policies insure against death and sickness, and those who can afford to take up all three insure against death, sickness and unemployment, but only in that order. What are the explanations
20　why they do not insure against all three? The first is that their wages are too low. I am talking now about the uninsured portion. Their wages are too low to enable them to insure against all three without some assistance. The second difficulty, and it is the greatest of all, is that during a period of sickness or unemployment, when they are
25　earning nothing, they cannot keep up the premiums. They may be able to do it for a fortnight or three weeks, but when times of very bad trade come, when a man is out of work for weeks and weeks at a time, arrears run up with the friendly societies, and when the man gets work, it may be at the end of two or three months, those are not
30　the first arrears which have to be met. There are arrears of rent, arrears of the grocery bill, and arrears for the necessaries of life. At any rate he cannot consider his friendly society only. The result is that a very considerable number of workmen find themselves quite unable to keep up the premiums when they have a family to look
35　after.
　　Undoubtedly there is another reason. It is no use shirking the fact that a proportion of workmen with good wages spend them in other ways, and therefore have nothing to spare with which to pay premiums to friendly societies. It has come to my notice, in many of
40　these cases, that the women of the family make most heroic efforts to keep up the premiums to the friendly societies, and the officers of friendly societies, whom I have seen, have amazed me by telling the proportion of premiums of this kind paid by women out of the very wretched allowance given them to keep the household together. I
45　think it is well we should look all the facts in the face before we come

to consider the remedy. What does it mean in the way of lapses? I
have inquired of friendly societies, and, as near as I can get at it, there
are 250,000 lapses in a year. That is a very considerable proportion of
the 6,000,000 policies. The expectation of life at twenty is, I think, a
50   little over forty years, and it means that in twenty years' time there
are 5,000,000 lapses; that is, people who supported and joined
friendly societies, and who have gone on paying the premiums for
weeks, months, and even years, struggling along, at last, when a
very bad time of unemployment comes, drop out and the premium
55   lapses. It runs to millions in the course of a generation. What does
that mean? It means that the vast majority of the working men of this
country at one time or other have been members of friendly
societies, have felt the need for provision of this kind and it is only
because they have been driven, sometimes by their own habits, but
60   in the majority of cases by circumstances over which they have no
control – to abandon their policies. That is the reason why, at the
present moment, not one half of the workmen of this country have
made any provision for sickness, and not one-tenth for
unemployment. I think it necessary to state these facts in order to
65   show that there is a real need for some system which would aid the
workmen over these difficulties. I do not think there is any better
method, or one more practicable at the present moment, than a
system of national insurance which would invoke the aid of the State
and the aid of the employer to enable the workman to get over all
70   these difficulties and make provision for himself for sickness, and,
as far as the most precarious trades are concerned, against
unemployment.

Lloyd George, Chancellor of the Exchequer, 4 May 1911,
Parliamentary Debates, 5th Series, vol 25, cols 611–13, quoted
in W. D. Handcock, op cit

Questions

a What was a 'friendly society' (line 28)?
b How expensive was insurance for all three provisions mentioned
by Lloyd George?
c Why did many policies lapse? What was the rate at which policies
lapsed?
d Who were most likely to try to keep up the insurance premiums?
Why was this so?
e In what 'other ways' (lines 37–8) do you think the men with good
wages spend their money?
f Did many working men think there was a real need for various
types of insurance?

13 Local Government Act, 1929

1. . . . the functions of each poor law authority, shall . . . be transferred to the council of the county or county borough.

6.(1) An administrative scheme shall provide for the constitution of a committee of the council (hereinafter referred to as the public assistance committee).

7.(1) In the case of a county the administrative shall provide
- (a) for the division of the county into areas and . . . for each such area of a local sub-committee of the public assistance committee (to be called the guardians committee).
- (c) for the discharge . . . of the following matters
  - (i) the consideration and examination of applications for relief;
  - (ii) the determination of the nature and amount of relief
  - (iii) the determination of the amount, if any, to be paid by any recipient of relief, . . . towards reimbursing the Council the amount expended by them on his relief
  - (iv) the visiting inspection or management . . . of any poor law institutions in the area.

Quoted in W. D. Handcock, op cit

Questions

a Do you consider the names of committees for enforcement of the law mentioned in 6(1) and 7(1) were well chosen?
b Was the procedure for obtaining relief substantially changed?
c Can you suggest reasons why the county and county borough councils were given these responsibilities?

Quoted in W. D. Handcock, op cit

14 Plus ça change, plus c'est la même chose

We understand that the poor law Acts and regulations made thereunder prohibit, except in special cases, the unconditional outdoor relief of able-bodied persons, and although the Minister of Health has found it necessary, during the extreme post-war depression, to assent to a widespread use of regulations permitting unconditional relief in special cases, we think, both from the point of view of the parties to the unemployment insurance and on general grounds, that in so far as it deals with the able-bodied unemployed, poor law relief should retain the deterrent effect which now attaches to it, or may be applied thereto.

Ministry of Labour, Report of the Departmental Committee (Blanesburgh) on Unemployment Insurance, 1927, quoted Marwick, A. *Britain in the Century of Total War* (Pelican, 1970) p 173

Questions

a   Why should the Committee want to retain the 'deterrent effect which now attaches' to poor law relief (line 9)?

b   Why should its retention be significant from the point of view of 'the parties to the unemployment insurance' (line 7)?

★ c   Had conditions in the early twentieth century proved the poor law relief system unworkable?

d   In what ways did the reorganisation of the Poor Law in 1834 inhibit the massive state interference that had occurred, for example, in education?